Good Girls

DON'T

FINISH

Felicia White

To all the good girls just waiting for your opportunity to live,
now is your time.

Preface

One night my girlfriends and I went to dinner after bible study. This was the special kind of night when my phone decided that it wanted to jump out of my lap and into the storm drain as I got out of the car and headed into the restaurant. This should have been a sign that things were about to get real. At dinner, conversations went from church to work to guys, of course. We talked about the difficulties of dating in general and dating while being a good girl with standards. The conversation was complete with the stories from recent dates that ranged from awkward to downright awful. Then, I brought up my pet peeve, which is when guys use the "nice guys finish last" mantra to sing the blues about why some girl didn't want to date them. I'd barely gotten the words out of my mouth when my friend loudly scoffed, "Hmph! Good girls don't finish!!" I was so shocked at her response that my eyes got so big! My friend that was sitting next to me "clutched her pearls" and turned her head with a pained expression.

What she said was exactly what I was getting at — good girls really seem to have it the hardest in the dating game, as well as in life in general. However, I had never heard it put quite like that. The boldness of the phrase was like a slap in the face. A reality check. That truth hurt. "Lord, God in Heaven, PLEASE NO!" we silently pleaded. Everyone at the table was taken aback. A collection of half thoughts spilled out of our mouths while we tried to pull ourselves together and continue the conversation. Meanwhile, I'm sure many of us were probably praying to God that the newfound expression wouldn't be our story. Even while writing this now, I feel an aftershock to the earthquake that shook my foundation a bit. Why is it that good girls, who presumably should be winning in their social and professional lives, are losing? More importantly, how can we change our reality?

Introduction

Hey girl! It's Friday night. You're at home catching up on the shows that you've missed during the week. Maybe you have friends over this week, but more than likely you're hanging out at home by yourself. It is just another monotonous week, just like the one before, and a foreshadowing of the week to come. You go to the kitchen to grab yet another snack to munch on while you aimlessly pass the time until eleven o'clock so you can go to bed. Eleven is late enough for you to say you were tired and had an "early night." You know, in case anyone actually asks. The recorded shows have all gone off, but there is still time to kill. So you turn on a marathon of reruns of your favorite reality trash. You check the 'Gram and your Snaps to see all the exciting things your friends are doing.

Silently, you judge some of your networks' poor decisions or at least their poor decision to actually post the ratchetness. But, of course, you would *never* say it to them. As you continue to scroll through your timeline, you are slightly envious of the events that others are attending. Then, you double tap that picture anyways to show them some love. You don't want to seem like a hater in real life. Mindlessly, you check Facebook and your Twitter feed. Nothing. Any new Snaps? Nope. Because you don't want to seem like you're at home bored, you take a picture of the snack wrappers, your legs under a cozy blanket, and your slippers on the floor in front of the couch. Then, you reluctantly post the image with the hashtags: *#MeTime. #AllllllTheSnacks! #TurnUpForWhat?* The pictures show that you *chose* to take the night off to relax. Duh.

After a while, there comes a point in the night where you begin to be introspective. How did you get to this point where every week is predictable? The only wild card will be if you're having pizza or Chinese food for dinner. You feel almost numb from the monotony of your life. Frustrated, you start to wonder why people don't think to invite you to certain events and why your phone is dry despite being full of numbers. You love your friends and family, and maybe even your job. However, you are desperate for passion in your life. The role of being the good girl that you once felt secure in, now feels constricting. It is hard to do certain things because you know people have high expectations for you, and you don't want to disappoint anyone. Furthermore, deep down inside, what you want the most is to know your purpose and live a life that is so much bigger than the box that you have been residing in for so many years. However, all you see is the same things you have always had. And, you have been living this life for so long that you have absolutely no idea how to change anything about it.

If you can relate to this scenario, this book is for you. This is a reminder that you can be sweet *and* ambitious. Being nice doesn't mean that everyone else's needs are always above yours. You can choose to prioritize your needs and still show love to family and friends. The greatest disservice that you can do to yourself is to never choose to actively work to pursue your passions. Nobody wants to grow old and full of regret, never having the opportunity to see what could have been. So don't! Decide to live life differently and follow through with your plans. Make yourself a priority for once. God has given every single individual a specific purpose. Like a seed that is planted, you have to water and nourish it, *especially* while it's taking root in the ground. You have no idea who needs you to be yourself or how your story may change someone's whole life. Hearing your story and experiencing your gift may be just what someone needs so that they can be inspired to take their own journey to the next level. While reading this book, be honest with yourself. Let your guard down. Write down in a notebook the things that speak to you. Keep an open mind. While some parts of this book are extremely direct, everything was written from a place of love. Be free to fully experience this life and every blessing that God wants you to have. Get out of your own way, and start living.

* * *

Note: This is not a dating and relationship book. The purpose of this book is not to learn how to get or keep a man. This goal of this book is for you to become confident enough, bold enough, and strong enough to leave the safety of your comfort zone and turn your potential into actual successes. It is about inspiring you to live your life in a way that reflects God's glory and will for your life. When you start to develop these character traits, they will cause transformations to occur in every part of your life. *Girl, get ready to finish!*

CHAPTER 1

Good Girls

What makes a "Good Girl"?

She is the woman who is constantly apologizing for menial things or issues far beyond her control. She's the indecisive teenager afraid to voice her opinion; the girl who genuinely can't accept a compliment because she lacks confidence and hates attention. For the purpose of this book, a good girl is a rule-following, refined woman who is unable to shine at her brightest potential because she has accepted the restrictive and small-minded beliefs of others as the standards to govern her life. This woman overthinks simple situations because she wants to make sure that absolutely no one will be offended by her actions. She has such a tight grip on her behavior and only allows herself to let loose around a select few; but even still, no one really knows her biggest and deepest dreams. She is kind of like spa water — a cucumber, mint, and lime mixture that is sophisticated and refreshing but lacking real flavor.

In this context, being a good girl doesn't necessarily mean that her morals are higher when compared to any other woman's standards. It is a mentality that manifests in her behavior. Being perceived as a good girl is important because this standard has infused itself into her identity. Over the years, this woman has been taught to think of her needs last while she works tirelessly for the needs of others. She dreams wholeheartedly, but she is terrified of stepping out on faith and making those dreams a reality. You have definitely met this girl. You've seen her characterized on TV. Unfortunately, she exists in every family. She may even be you.

When I think of the women typically classified as good girls, there are certain characteristics that they all seem to have. Again, it's not that these women necessarily have higher morals, but there is a social commonality in the way that they think and interact with people. From a young age, many girls are encouraged to fit themselves into this cookie cutter image of how a lady should think, speak, and behave. They are told not to be too loud or opinionated; don't be aggressive or assertive. They are encouraged to have certain types of clothes, make up, and physiques that are appropriate for upstanding women. They tend to get involved in the same activities that are the norm for everyone else in their family or social group. Largely, they are women who have developed a pattern of letting people make decisions for them, either consciously or subconsciously. They don't ruffle any feathers, and these good girls don't challenge the status quo. They seamlessly fit nicely into the neat little predictable boxes that put people at ease.

This concept goes against the grain a bit because being a good girl is still praised by the majority, and understandably so. Theoretically, this woman makes the perfect wife and mother because she gives selflessly of all that she has for those who need her. She makes the perfect employee because she follows instructions to the letter. She is the best friend because she is always available to listen to the problems of others and offer calm, rational, reasonable advice. She'll even give this advice multiple times since the people asking her for it aren't typically calm, rational, or reasonable, and they never take her advice the first time. This all sounds great. And, for the most part, it is. However, for most women, too often the cost of being perfect for everyone else is the inability to prioritize personal needs.

As an employee, she sometimes misses opportunities for promotion because she has never shown her creativity and critical thinking skills. This was because she was so focused on exhibiting the exact expectations of her employers. Maybe it could have been because they believe that her passive nature means that she would be ill-equipped for upper-management. When it comes time to get a raise or request the minimum salary that she will accept at a new job, she's so uncomfortable that she low-balls her offer. She does this so that the employer isn't offended by her asking for too much, instead of demanding what she's worth. With friends and family, she is at times taken for granted, and her generosity is taken advantage of because people know that she will do what is requested of her in order to avoid confrontation. While good girls possess seemingly admirable qualities, if they are ever going to make it to the finish line and eventually begin to win, their perspectives must change. They have to rediscover their hidden interests and fight for dreams to come true while juggling current responsibilities. Or, they must drop some of the current responsibilities that no longer serve them and decide that fulfilling their purpose is more important than being an extra in someone else's dreams.

New Year, Same You

Every year, most people do a personal evaluation and think of the progress that they have made in various areas of their life. Most times, it's not by choice. The New Year and birthdays seem to come with a side of self-reflection. We are abruptly confronted by the passing of time. Career paths, friendships, dreams, and romantic relationships are all analyzed and reevaluated, which is great because it keeps us on track and gives perspective. Unfortunately, if you are anything like me, there are at least a handful of glaringly obvious items that you swore last year would be completed by now. In fact, they are things that really should have been crossed off the list two years ago.

After evaluating the course your life has taken over the past couple of years, you get really frustrated and upset with your lack of progress. You may even blame it on those last few months *flying* by. However, if you were to be completely honest, when was the last time that you actively made yourself stick to your plans? When was the last time you even created plans, instead of just throwing together generic goals for the year? When was the last time you actually planned to do something to better yourself physically, mentally, financially, or spiritually just because it was what you needed to do for yourself? The goals could have been anything that would make you better — the new healthy lifestyle that you wanted to create, taking that summer class to increase your knowledge base for work, or booking the trip to the country that you've always wanted to visit. And, what about your dreams? When was the last time you set time aside to work toward the things that you want most in the world? Did you follow through with those plans? How many goals are stacking up on the other side of tomorrow because you never make the decision to follow through with it? You'll never be able to finish if you never even start.

Do you even remember who you always wanted to be before adulting got the best of you and before you began letting everyone else's responsibilities take precedence in your life? So often, good girls find it hard to stray from the beaten path that the world has deemed safe, responsible, and respectable. They crave the validation from both authority figures and peers, even as adults. They avoid confrontation and controversial topics to keep from ever offending anyone. It is an internal struggle between the person they really are and the person they feel pressured to remain. Still, after doing so for a while, they start to lose what is special and unique about themselves so that they fit the standard issued expectations of a lady. They indefinitely put their dreams on the shelf and spend most of their time watching other people live their lives. Meanwhile, they are settling for just living vicariously through others.

Unfortunately, this leaves an emptiness inside. There's a piece of you that will never be filled by another person or any material thing in this world. Your purpose begs to be fulfilled. It nags at you in those quiet moments because you know deep down that there is so much more that you could be doing. There's so much more that you need to do.

We are all different, and our purpose is very specific and individualized. We each have something special that we bring to the table. It is something that can change our families, community, or even the whole world, and it was birthed in each of us. Can you remember what it is? Do you feel it longing to manifest itself in your life? It's probably that idea that always pops up and you have hundreds of excuses as to why it won't work or why the timing isn't right. God is very intentional. His purpose for you is not something that He is creating as He goes. It is also not something that He is holding over your head just out of arms reach. He already placed it inside of you before you were born. It is probably something that you find yourself doing all of the time. Something that comes so naturally for you that it confuses you why other people can't do it. Seek God for a greater revelation of your purpose. Even though it is birthed in you, the final destination of where God is taking you will be far bigger than anything that you could have ever expected. It is so important to really understand who you are in God if you want to get the courage to run after your dreams at full speed and to break through the cycle and finally start completing your goals.

Sometimes it feels like everyone around you is doing so much better than you are. More than likely, they really aren't. They probably feel just as lost and unfulfilled as you do at times. Nobody really wants to share their most vulnerable and insecure feelings about their inadequacies. Unfortunately, far too few people take the necessary steps that are required to live a purposeful life. Not many people want to break the mold and be originals.

Now is your time to finish. Those what-ifs can't live in you forever. You must either go for it and find out what will happen, or eventually those what-ifs will turn into "I wish I would have" and "It could have been me." And, to be clear, when I say finish, I don't mean after you have done everything you've ever thought of doing. I just mean I want you to start collecting victories, no matter how small at first. Complete something to get the ball rolling towards your goal so that you believe you can be a finisher.

I've never run track before, but I imagine you first start off with races with other people wanting to try out for the team. Then, if you do well enough, you make the team. After that, during practice, you race teammates who will keep you on your game. Then, you start racing kids from other schools and so on until you go to the state championship. Each level you accomplish, no matter how small the margin, is a win. That's finishing. Then, you start the next goal that you have to finish. It's a continually repeating cycle until our time here is up. Our goal is to do the best that we can and trust God with the rest. Take that first step. Then, take the next step. Before you know it, you've finished more than you ever thought was possible. And, trust me, that's something you'll never regret.

Been There, Done That

I know it seems like I just started attacking the sweet little good girls right out of the gate. But, I understand the how it feels to be so concerned with the opinions of others that I'm paralyzed with indecision. I've been through periods of being so bored with my life because I only did what was expected of me. Despite knowing all that I was capable of, I limited my behaviors to things that I thought would offend the least amount of people. Whether or not I actually asked for advice, I took all of the opinions of others into consideration based on my past experiences with them. I was frustrated because I saw other people living these amazing lives and having incredible opportunities, while my life never seemed to change. Year after year went by as I spent time just waiting for something new to come into my life. Finally, one day, the realization smacked me in the face that God was not going to just do everything for me. I had a role to play. In order for me to receive the blessings that God already promised, I had to do the work. It required trusting in God and having active faith. I had to decide to take God at His word and be an active participant in my own life if I really wanted to fulfill my purpose.

I was raised a church girl — a preacher's kid to be specific. I always made the honor roll, and then I consistently made the Dean's List in college. I became campus queen my senior year of college. I was your quintessential good girl. While in most families the youngest child seems to have the least amount of structure, growing up as the youngest of three had the opposite effect on me. I made a conscious effort not to do things that would get me in trouble. Therefore, I followed instructions, kept to myself, and didn't stir the pot. If it seemed to have the possibility of me creating contention, I avoided it like the plague. I didn't want to make mistakes or accept any risks. I wanted to excel at everything so that I didn't disappoint other people. But, I found out the hard way that there are two major problems with living like this: it doesn't work, and you lose yourself in the process.

People are fickle little creatures. It is impossible to live a life that does not disappoint anyone. The things that they loved yesterday, they are indifferent to today. The jokes that made them laugh at lunch, they now find annoying. It is a never-ending, losing battle trying to base your decisions and life choices on a person or group of people, no matter how much you love them. You will end up angry and aggravated by trying to fulfill their never-ending list of requirements. And, since you feel like they depend on you to do certain things, you keep running in circles for them. All the while, they are rarely appreciative, and usually they don't notice the time and effort that you expended to accomplish the tasks. Of course, they never run out of items on the to-do list. What it comes down to is most people are looking out for their own best interest. This is not to say that everyone is inherently bad or immoral, because that is not true. These acts can be done either consciously or subconsciously. Still, in an effort to accomplish their goals, they want people who will consistently give time and resources toward their own interests. Some people are drawn to people pleasers — people who have a hard time saying no. Good girls.

Women are notorious for taking care of everyone else's needs. We empathize with people, and we are natural nurturers. Therefore, it comes second-nature to us to do things that will make the people we love happy and comfortable. As we get older, the number of people we love grows. We meet more friends, we get into romantic relationships that lead to marriage, and then one day we may even have children. These are all really great things, but this means that time and resources get stretched more and more. It is crucial to intentionally make time for personal needs and goals. If you fail to do so, it is easy for your needs to be forgotten over time. I understand that sometimes you simply don't have the time to do what you love on a given day. However, if day after day and month after month, you consistently don't make time for yourself and your needs, you slowly start to lose the person you used to be.

Meanwhile, you just continue doing what your closest friends or family like to do, and you just go with the flow. Then one day, years later, you can barely think of things that you personally enjoy. You don't remember when everything changed. More than ever before, you question your purpose in this life. This is one of the worst feelings. I've been there. There is a disconnection between the person that you have become and the person you are called to be, and you don't know how to reconnect. It is necessary to remember that you were not put on this earth for the sole purpose of helping everyone else achieve their dreams. You matter. It is time to set boundaries and enforce them. This is your life, and you only get one. Don't waste it.

It doesn't matter whether you are a single woman who is only taking care of herself, a married mother, or any status in between. Now is the perfect time in your life to focus on creating a life that you love that connects with your God-given purpose. It is *always* the perfect time to actively work for your dreams. Arriving safely at death is not a notable accomplishment. There will always be responsibilities. There will always be excuses not to do it. However, there will not always be more time. So stop playing safe and start winning at life. There are no prizes for being a person that everyone likes if you never fulfill your calling in the end. Decide what you want to do, set goals, and follow through. Give yourself the opportunity to acknowledge and live out your dreams. Be more than just a game changer; be a *life* changer.

Authentic

*"If you're content to simply be yourself,
your life will count for plenty."*

MATTHEW 23:12 MSG

CHAPTER 2

Real

Our generation is obsessed with being real. We crave genuine connections with our peers and expect honesty and transparency in authority figures, politicians, and even celebrities. Even with all of that, the majority of us somehow have a hard time being vulnerable and showing our real selves to the world. Being vulnerable in this world feels pretty similar to handing your worst enemy a flash drive full of the worst things you have ever done in your life so they can post it online. It leaves us feeling completely exposed. The mere thought of it is enough to convince most of us to bury ourselves deeper into the warm comforts of the status quo. Then, you find yourself stuck in a no-win situation where all you crave is authenticity from the people around you, but you can never really get what you're looking for because you are not living authentically yourself. It is impossible to effectively connect to people because your own heart is completely guarded and hidden away.

This phenomenon is even worse for the good girls. After years and years of putting their wants and needs after the desires of parents, church leaders, professors, boyfriends, and other friends, many good girls don't even really know who they are anymore. They feel like it is selfish to spend too much time doing things for themselves and exploring their own interests. The truth is that many are afraid to be themselves because the reality of who they are currently and who they desire to be is lightyears away from the woman that people *believe* they are and should be. The need to become the woman they were called to be battles with the desire to appease family and friends. Unfortunately, since they've been catering to the needs of those around them for such a long time, appeasing others is the side that continues to win the battle over and over again.

At the end of the day, it comes down to something very simple. What do you really believe? God gave you a voice. He crafted a unique perspective and vision when He created you. He gave you gifts as well as a purpose. Do you believe that? If so, how are you utilizing the gifts that you have been given? Everything that God gives you is an investment into you. There are people in this world who need the ideas and creations that come from the gifts that you have. If you are not operating in faith, who are you benefitting? How can you claim to be a child of the Most High God and choose to be small? It doesn't make sense to believe that God can do anything, and simultaneously believe that you cannot be successful in pursuing the desires of your heart. Especially, when He has already said otherwise.

What are you going to believe? That belief will become a reality in your life whether it is good or bad. That is how powerful you are. Challenge yourself to do something purposeful. Get out of your comfort zone and do something that you have always wanted to do yet you never had the nerve to try. Now is your time to develop into the full person you are created to be. As people age, they naturally get more cautious and reserved. So if you don't get the nerve to do it now, you may never go through with it.

Speak Up or Be Spoken For

Personally, one of my biggest pet peeves is being spoken for. I don't like when people try to explain on my behalf what they think that I think or feel, especially when I am there to speak for myself. I definitely don't like it when people try to talk over me simply because they naturally speak louder than I do. I don't even like when people try to finish my sentences. I think it's extremely disrespectful. This is especially true if it involves spending my money. On the surface, for the most part, I am friendly and laidback. Because of this, people with more aggressive personality types would make decisions and assume that I would just go along with whatever was decided. Unfortunately, for far too long I would do just that. I would be angry and irritated, but I thought that it was rude to choose not to participate after the plans had been made. I thought that because they'd made the plans assuming a set number of people would be there to split the bill, it made me look like the bad guy to make everyone pay more if I opted out of participating.

The older I got, the more it bothered me when people failed to request my input. I began to ask myself why I was spending my time with certain people if they didn't think enough of me as a person to attempt to understand my point of view. Then, I admitted to myself that it was time to start reevaluating relationships and making cuts! However, I still had to ask myself why they felt like it was okay to continue to speak for me. The reality was that even though I had such strong perspectives, I was so guarded that I had never given others the opportunity to get to know me fully. They never even knew there was a problem because I stewed internally, and then eventually got over it. Therefore, I had to take ownership of helping to create this issue. I had to speak up and explain my point of view. Until I made the decision to be more vulnerable with people, they would never have had the ability to be a good friend to me.

Is there an area in your life where you don't feel like you are being heard? Are you being honest with the people around you about what is important to you? You have to recognize the value of your point of view. The inability to speak up for what is important comes from a skewed perspective of self-worth. It comes from not really believing what God has said about you. If you don't think that your opinion is respected, or you are just too timid to verbally state how you feel, it is easy to drift to the background where no one will ever even ask. In fact, that may be what you are hoping will happen so the weight and responsibility of what is discussed doesn't fall on you. However, if you are a Christian, you aren't called to be in the background. Of course everybody's role isn't to be a mega superstar preacher, but your assignment is too important for it to remain hidden.

> *"Ye are the light of the world.*
> *A city that is set on a hill cannot be hid."*
> Matthew 5:14, KJV

In this scripture, the comparison to light really takes away your ability to hide your gifts. In a pitch black room, a light, no matter how dim, will be seen. It's a pitch black world. People are looking for answers and you are the one who has that answer for someone.

Finding Your Voice

So often, good girls are walking around telling people that they are looking for their voice or trying to find the *right* way to proceed that will not offend anyone or hurt anyone's feelings. Really stop and think about what is being said though. You already have a voice. Everyone does. Yet, for some reason you believe that your voice is not good enough. Meanwhile, you definitely have opinions and a unique perspective on things. There are specific things that bother you in a way that it doesn't seem to bother other people.

There are things that you find inspirational that others see as useless information. Think of the conversations that you have with your closest friends. Pay attention to what makes you uncomfortable or excited. What are the things that naturally cause you to have strong reactions?

If you feel the need to *find* your voice, you may not know yourself as well as you should. In all honesty, you may not even know God the way that you should. Again, it comes down to what you believe. Do you believe that God created you voiceless and purposeless and makes you wait decades before He will give you something to say? I don't. I believe that many people have doubts or lack confidence and allow others to override what God is saying to them. Over the course of time, they rely more and more on those opinions of others because they can no longer make decisions for themselves and have completely tuned out the voice of God in their lives.

One major thing that surprised me the first time I really read the gospels was that Jesus Christ was bold. He challenged people to understand ancient principles in new ways. Often when people asked Him questions, He responded back with questions or parables. On many occasions, the Pharisees tried to manipulate His words and would leave frustrated because they couldn't. He would not allow them to put Him into the safe little box that fit their level of understanding. Jesus was clear about His mission. He didn't allow people who didn't want to hear what He had to say distract Him from it. Even the disciples were not exempt from it because they were close to Him.

"Jesus turned and said to Peter, 'Get behind me, Satan!
You are a stumbling block to me; you do not have in mind
the concerns of God, but merely human concerns.'"
Matthew 16:23, NIV

People try to recreate the image of Jesus as someone who was passive and non-confrontational. However, Jesus rebuked Peter who was in His inner circle when he tried to speak against Him fulfilling His purpose. It is possible to love someone and create boundaries for them, and it is okay to protect your dreams from people who try to deter you from doing what you know you need to do. Verbalize your opinions. Express your point of view. It is possible that people may not like what you have to say. They may get upset with how you respond. In fact, they may be annoyed that you responded, and that's perfectly fine. Since people aren't used to you speaking up, it may take them a while to adjust to you. That's normal. Remember that when people complain about how you speak, it's usually more about their insecurities than something that you did. The only thing that you can do is respond in love. You aren't responsible for how they perceive what you said. Think about the last time someone told you no. It didn't really matter how it was said; it just didn't feel good to hear because it was not what you wanted to hear. Saying it nicely doesn't take the sting out when someone is upset that they aren't getting their way. Still, try not to let their offense send you right back into your old habits.

The thing to remember is that while some people may not like what you have to say, the critics are usually in the minority. There are going to be many more that love your point of view. You may be able to verbalize something that they have always felt but didn't know how to express. There will be people that you inspire; people who are drawn to you and can't wait to hear what you say next. This is because people are drawn to the light, and authenticity is attractive in the purest sense. So few people are confident enough to speak their minds and be genuine that when one does, others can't help but pay attention. Even amongst your friends and family, they will be even more proud that they can say that they know you. The people who love you want you to be yourself. So even though there will always be critics of anyone who has an opinion, the positivity that you receive will be more than worth it. Be confident in what you have to say. Your words have power. People will behave according to what you allow.

The Ideal Customer

Did you know that companies use studies about human interactions in order to optimize their product sales? So when you walk by the kiosk salesmen in the mall selling $100 skin care products, *but for you I'll sell it for $40,* they use your natural desire to not offend against you. They try to engage you with questions and address you individually so it makes you feel rude to breeze by. Once they've stopped you, they rub five types of creams on your hand and you pretend to be wowed by the difference that it makes. You keep trying to make excuses to leave, but there's always *one more thing* that they want you to try. Then, when they ask you to buy, there is a really uncomfortable conversation in which they do not accept your refusals. This goes to the point when you actually start contemplating buying something just so you can leave. It is the same concept that a lot of people use in their daily interactions.

This happens regularly, not just with the kiosk salesmen, but also with the people walking the streets downtown asking you to sign petitions and donate money to dozens of causes and with people at school, work, or church who want you to take the lead on a volunteer project that everyone thought was a good idea but no one has time to organize. Some also see it in their family members who need one more favor, one more time. You don't want to offend them, but they are taking no consideration of your needs or feelings. These people know that they can wear most people down and get what they want, even if you are only doing it to get out of the conversation.

It is easy to spot the people who have a hard time saying no.

These are the people who end up doing the entire group project because the group members know that person is reliable and they'll make a good grade. Those are the people that group leaders go to when they really want some things done and don't want to spend a whole bunch of time looking for helpers. However, over time, this is unfortunately how people who naturally want to help begin to feel used. They become overworked, and their desire to participate diminishes until they dread being a part of the group at all.

Does this person sound familiar? What can fix this problem? Start by speaking up for yourself. All too often, good girls find it difficult to confront people because they don't want to hurt anyone's feelings. Meanwhile, they are being hurt by the situation. It is okay to address the issue. The situation will never change until you change it. Everyone else is benefitting from it while you're fighting an internal battle. It is your responsibility to set the standards for how you are treated. Similarly, when you are dating a guy, you have clear expectations for how he will treat you. If he doesn't meet that standard, you address it. If it continues, you rethink the relationship. However, if you never create any standards, it leaves you open to be treated however he feels is best. His actions will be based on his previous relationships with women, which may or may not reflect your true value. Once you have decided that your needs are worth standing up for, other people will have no choice but to follow suit or else they'll be left behind.

CHAPTER 3

God Doesn't Need Another Cookie Cutter Christian

"Now there are diversities of gifts, but the same Spirit.
And there are differences of administrations, but the same
Lord. And there are diversities of operations, but it is the
same God which worketh all in all."

1 Corinthians 12:4–6, KJV

In society, an expectation is placed on women to live and behave a specific way. This is especially true for women in the church. Growing up, women are taught to be still and quiet, look presentable but dress conservatively, and to submit and obey. They are told to be ladylike. In itself, these aren't bad things; it teaches young girls how to regulate themselves. However, it can possibly prevent them from fully learning themselves. And potentially, it prevents them from learning how to express themselves as Christians as well as individuals. Not everyone can fit the strict requirements of being considered ladylike. Some people are just loud, antsy, and opinionated; it's just their personality.

The personality is a part of how people were created, as are the thoughts and the unique point of view. God is very creative. There is no reason that God would make you one way or with certain traits, and then require that you completely change to a dull duplicated version of every other woman. Granted, there are some parts of your character that must be developed. He expects that our lives will reflect the fruit of the Spirit. However, the same fruit can be expressed in a myriad of ways. How many types of apples have you seen in the grocery stores? There are Fuji, gala, honey crisp, McIntosh, granny smith, and so many more. While they each have different characteristics, they are all apples. Each type of apple has noticeable unique variations that can easily be seen on the surface level such as size and color differences, but they also vary greatly in their tastes.

Similarly, we are able to look and think differently while striving ultimately toward one goal. We will have different approaches to living our life for God, because if God wanted us to be robots, He could have easily created us that way. There is a reason for giving us freewill and creating individuals. You are crafted with a specific personality, with specific gifts, and to reach a specific subset of people. And, that won't happen if you are forcing yourself to change in a way that God has not directed. The arbitrary standards that society has set may not work for you. Break the mold. "Wide is the gate, and broad is the way, that leadeth to destruction." (Matthew 7:13, KJV) Don't follow the crowd. God told you to go, so go! The journey to your destiny is not going to look like anyone else's because you aren't like anyone else. And you aren't necessarily going where they are going. Be bold enough to follow God on your own path, "because strait is the gate, and narrow is the way, which leadeth unto life, and few there be that find it." (Matthew 7:14) Only few find it! Not everyone is living life this way. Unfortunately, not every Christian is really living a life that is full of faith. The people that you look to for guidance should be people who are actively working to fulfill their purpose. If they never attempted to achieve their dreams, they probably aren't suitable mentors. The narrow gate means that everyone can't go with you. Know that if you have faith you can be everything that God designed you to be, which is so much more than you could even imagine.

What is God leading you to do? What are the desires of your heart? Maybe you want to move to a new city. You feel cramped, and there is nowhere left for you to grow where you live. Relocate. Find cities that have prominent industries for the passions that you have. Study abroad for new experience or to increase your cultural awareness. If you are being called to start a business, open a community center, or write a book, get to it! There's no better time than the present. God is so big. This world is full of so many different types of people, and it has tons of individual needs. God can use your desires for His glory, and He can show you what you are capable of when you trust in Him. "If the whole body were an eye, where were the hearing? If the whole were hearing, where were the smelling? (1 Corinthians 12:17, KJV)" The body does not function optimally when everyone arbitrarily discards who they were created to be because they think it's not good enough. Be confident in who God has made you. Recognize that your individuality is needed.

Free Your Mind

> *"Now the Lord is that Spirit: and where*
> *the Spirit of the Lord is, there is liberty."*
> 2 Corinthians 3:17, KJV

I would argue that everyone is born free. Babies operate on their own schedule. As they become toddlers, they are able to speak and behave in whatever way seems best to them in that moment. Their parents then begin to teach them acceptable ways to speak and behave for their culture and environment. This is absolutely necessary for successful societies to continue. However, the individuality and creativity that comes from being completely free is necessary in order to bring the best advancements for society as a whole. Unfortunately, in the process of becoming a productive member of society, many people lose their individuality and forget the fact that they are still free to work toward their dreams.

A long time ago, I heard a story about training elephants in a circus. I've never spoken to elephant trainers personally to know if this is their process, but let's assume it's true. The trainers would take a captured baby elephant and tie its tail to a stake of some sort in the center of a room. This is so it could only move within a given circumference within the room. The elephant would tug and pull against it because no living being naturally wants to live even a single moment in confinement. Unfortunately, it is not able to get away. As the elephant gets bigger, the trainers replace the stake and still keep the elephant tied up. Finally, after the elephant matures into its full size, the trainers untie its tail from the stake. Surprisingly though, the elephant no longer tries to get away! It is much bigger and stronger than any person in the room, but its mind has been enslaved. It has been trained to view itself as being less powerful than it really is.

This is the way too many of us live our lives. We know the circle. It is comfortable. The circle is safe. We can pay our bills just fine, and everyone likes us. We don't want to risk our stability and ultimately our lives and livelihoods for a "pipe dream." Whether that is moving forward on a business idea, going for a promotion at work, or creating a neighborhood program, we want to have complete control over our lives in every aspect. Letting go of your current circumstance for your future potential is definitely a risk, in theory. However, in reality, God will always bless the situation when you are completing the purpose that He designed you for, so there really is no risk at all — only fear.

> *"Stand fast therefore in the liberty wherewith Christ hath made us free, and be not entangled again with the yoke of bondage."*
> Galatians 5:1, KJV

Over the course of our lives, we are constantly being influenced by our family, friends, schools, churches, and media. People, now more than ever, publicly give unsolicited advice on every topic imaginable to anyone who will listen. You will also notice that the people who receive the most criticism are the ones who are bold enough to stand on their convictions and do what they believe is best, whether they are actually right or wrong. The thing is, criticism is unavoidable if you want to live an influential and purposeful life. Even the nicest celebrities in the world are criticized for not being *strong* enough or for being *too nice* in their responses to situations. Regardless, at some point you have to decide if you are actually going to do what you are called to do. What is it worth to you? Do the opinions of others mean so much to you that you will forfeit your destiny? Hopefully, the answer is no. But, do your actions confirm what you are saying?

It's not always easy at first. It took me a very long time to start saying what I wanted to accomplish. There was a feeling of vulnerability when I spoke my heart's desires, so I just kept it to myself. I didn't want people to know and judge me by whether or not I acted on my dreams. Furthermore, I didn't even want to say it aloud when I was alone because it made it real. It made me think about all the things that I could be doing to reach the goal, as well as all of the things that I am doing currently that are really just self-sabotaging. When I kept it to myself, there was no responsibility to follow through with anything. However, I was miserable because the life I was living was vastly different from the one I knew that I was capable of living. It wasn't until I began really seeking God that my mentality changed, and I began behaving like someone who really trusts God with everything.

Don't believe the lie that you are unworthy. Don't believe that you are not capable of fulfilling your dreams. God is able to do anything, and He wouldn't have given you that specific dream for a specific thing that this world needs. There is a reason why other people don't understand your vision. They can't see what you see because it isn't their assignment. You have to challenge yourself to step out on faith long enough to get the ball rolling. Once it starts, it will be easy to believe for bigger and better. The longer you wait and the more you tell yourself that you are inadequate, the harder it will be to begin. Audibly tell yourself that you can do whatever God has placed you here to do. Say it every morning and every evening until you believe it. Yell it if you must. You have to fight for your destiny and believing that you can is the first step.

If you are reading this book, you quite likely live in a free society where you are able to do anything that you are inspired to do. You have access to the most up to date information in the world and more easily accessible forms of technology. It has never been this easy to create your own opportunity in the history of the whole world. No matter what happened in your past, you have the ability to change your whole world simply by making the decision to do so. It *is* that easy. Believe it. That is all that it takes to change your mindset and give it everything today. There are no excuses.

Walk Confidently

*"Remember this, and do not abandon your confidence, which will
lead to rich rewards. Simply endure, for when you have done as God
requires of you, you will receive the promise."*

Hebrews 10:35–36, The VOICE

Body language is your messy best friend that tells all of your
business. It conveys whether you are confident, bashful, tired, or
frantic. A woman may be wearing a beautiful outfit, but because
she is hunched over or hiding behind someone, people can tell
that she is not very confident. Think about how you felt the last
time you wore a skirt that rises up when you walk or a dress that is
a little tighter than you normally wear. You're constantly shifting
things all day so you look presentable; however, you feel, and *look*,
uncomfortable. Similarly, people notice confidence through your
body language in every aspect of your life. When you are confident,
people can see that you know your value, and they tend to give you
the benefit of the doubt. For example, if you are hiring and two
candidates are sitting next to each other. One is sitting up straight,
smiling, and making eye contact, while the other is fidgeting in her
chair, clammy, and looking nervous. You would already be leaning
toward the first candidate because she looks like she believes that
she is capable of being successful not only in the interview, but also
in the position.

The truest feelings that you have toward yourself are displayed
through your daily interactions. Ensure that your thoughts and
beliefs toward yourself are those of confidence and power. Let your
very presence make people aware that you know your value. In
doing so, it teaches people how to treat you and what to expect
from you. When people make reservations at a five-star restaurant,
they show up on time, wear elegant attire, and they plan to spend

money. They know that the restaurant has standards and that they can get turned away for not dressing appropriately, even if they have the money to eat there. However, the restaurant stays in business because the quality of food and staff are worth the price. They know their value, and they hold you to their standards. Walk like you have dominion over your circumstance, because you do.

Value yourself. Don't wait for everyone else to decide that you are worth it. Do you know God's opinions of you? Do you realize how much He really loves you? You are His child. What good father wants his child to feel worthless, incompetent, or unloved? Not one. A great father sees the best potential in their child and wants their child to be successful. See yourself through God's eyes and act accordingly. No one on this earth will want it for you more than you want it for yourself. No one can do the work for you. This is your life and your opportunity to be exceptional, living life with God's best – but, only if you believe that you can.

CHAPTER 4

Broken People

Unfortunately, we have all have experienced hurt in one form or another. Some struggle to overcome the effects of traumatic events, while others are trying to mend their hearts from past issues of rejection and feelings of unworthiness. Having problems does not make you less than others, because everyone has had them. However, don't allow those past experiences to become excuses as to why you are unable to go to the next level. As much as it hurt and as much work as it will require to get through it, you have to push forward. You've already survived the experience. Thank God! Don't let your emotions keep you permanently shackled. Don't let your past ruin your future. What happened may not have been something that you could have changed because you had no control over it. However, going forward, it is your choice on how you will learn and excel from that experience. Choosing not to forgive and holding on to the hurt and bitterness will only weigh you down.

There may be underlying issues that you need to address if there are dreams deep in your spirit that you want to achieve more than anything, but you have been putting them off for years. Whether you are afraid of being rejected, you feel unworthy, or you are just afraid, think of what the root of those feelings could be. It doesn't really make sense that the thing that we want the most is the thing that we are most afraid to go after. Pray. Do the work, because nothing is worth your freedom or your future. Also, know that God is a healer. He's a deliverer. Find comfort in His word. Talk about it with someone that you love. And, for more intense or traumatic issues, talk to someone with professional counseling experience. The hidden and heavily guarded secret of your past loses its power over you when you vocalize your experiences. Learn new ways to process any triggers that you may have so you can grow from it. Reflect on your past, as ugly as it might be, and use it to become even better.

When Helping them is Hurting You

As we mature, we begin to outgrow things — friendships, jobs, maybe even a particular city as a whole. It is completely natural. A toddler has nutritional requirements that are different from those of a full grown adult. As that toddler grows, her appetite increases, and she begins to desire more. This holds true for our desires in our lives. Life is seasonal, so some things will complement each other during one phase of your life and cause friction in the next. On the other hand, you will completely outgrow some things altogether. Some amazing childhood friendships become toxic relationships as adults, unnecessarily chaining you to your past issues and mistakes. As difficult as it may be, there comes a point when some people have to leave your life. You may need to quit the job that you have been working for five years because in it, you are unable to continue growing. You may even have to move to another region in order to access the resources that you will need for what is next. Recognizing the issue and making the necessary cuts from your life can be difficult. Nostalgia builds up, and memories of the good times can cloud our judgment and prevent us from moving forward.

Analyze the relationship. Is it mutually beneficial? Do they support your vision? Can you trust them with your vision? Do you have the opportunity to grow and develop other gifts at your current job, church, or even in your town? Do you avoid the situation when possible and dread it when it's not? As a good girl, it can be even more difficult to break those ties because it usually involves being direct and confronting the issue head on. We don't want to seem mean and hurt others feelings. We don't want them to assume that we think that we are better than they are or leave people hanging if they rely on us. It is easy to convince yourself that this situation is a test or challenge that God has given you, so you just have to stick with it. But, is it really God, or is it just continued out of tradition? Why would God assign you to a place or to people that hurt your purpose? Some hard times strengthen your resolve and teach you how to fight, but there are others that you are meant to remove yourself.

God is a loving Father. He doesn't require His children to remain in abusive environments. He doesn't approve of people being manipulative, coercive, or oppressive in their words or actions toward you. It is important to remember that God gave each of us free will. Be cautious of any person who tries to use their authority or dominant personality to manipulate or control you inappropriately. However, God will put people in your life who will encourage or convict you as needed. Still, it is not done in a way that is oppressive. It is done in a way that reminds you of what God told you to do initially and brings you closer to Him. Ask God to help you discern the difference, and cut ties with the dead or damaging weight.

Many times, it's the good girls who are guilty of being people pleasers who can't step out because they feel like everyone else needs something from them. However, there are some good girls who are the clingers. They enjoy the comforts and familiarity with the people that they know and want it to stay exactly as it is currently. These women love so hard that it becomes constricting. They are hurt easily when people have a difference of opinion, and feel completely abandoned if someone wants to leave. Most times they have the best of intentions, but it is difficult to see past their very real, very intense emotions.

If this is more like you, pray that God will heal the hurts that you have experienced. Love shouldn't be confining. It should be freeing, like God Himself. Release them of the responsibility of being your everything. Sometimes God needs to remove old people and situations from your life so that you can grow from the experience, and so you will be in the proper position to receive new gifts and assignments. For example, you may have a favorite pair of shorts that are perfect to wear all summer long. If you continue to wear them into the fall, you may be able to get by without any major complications. However, when winter comes around with its freezing temperature wind chill, wearing those shorts will prevent you from retaining body heat and will make you sick. No matter how much you love it, if the season is over, let it go so it doesn't hinder your progress. Once you do, you'll have room to receive what you need for the next phase of life.

Deliverance from People

It is hard not to care. We are connected to not only the dozens of people that we love and interact with on a daily basis but also the hundreds — if not thousands — of contacts through social media full of people from our past and present. Each individual has a specific and limited view of who you are. These people may know things that you've done in your past that you'd rather forget. Depending on how close they are, they may have expectations of your future. Sometimes, we internalize the things that we *think* that they think about us. The things that we say, do, wear, and the places that we go are all too often heavily influenced by what everyone else thinks. (Or, in most cases, what we think they think.) What's more is that we are even concerned with the opinions of the people that we don't know who might see us and form an opinion about us or what we are doing. How much time is left to live your life if before making a decision you have to confer with a team of friends and family, and after you make the decision you have to do a debrief?

If you are trying to please everyone everywhere, you are going to fail every time. Evaluate the relationships that you have, and when you need it, only take advice from select people who have your best interest at heart. Overall though, you have to be confident in your decision-making ability. Exercise your own ability to discern situations, trust God, and learn to make the decision without the input of so many others.

One day I went over to a friend's house because I was so completely full of doubt and so frustrated with my situation. I shared with her that God told me to leave a particular place where I'd been for little over a year. I decided to follow through because I felt like God's instruction was very clear. I went to inform people of my decision, and after speaking to them, I felt very confused as to how I should proceed. Everything that they said sounded logical and plausible, and it made me doubt the message that I received. After I was done venting, my friend stopped and looked at me. She said, "You know this God. He is the same God you knew as a child. You know what He told you to do. Don't let someone who you have only known a few years make you doubt what you heard God say when you've known Him all of your life. Informing them was a nice thing to do, but what you are going to do is not really up for discussion." When she said that, I realized that she was right. The opinions of other people did not change what God so clearly told me to do. Of course, those people weren't trying to tell me to disobey God. They were trying to make sure that I wasn't making a rash decision. I should have been the one to definitively stand on what I had heard. It made me realize that I needed to have more confidence in my decisions and trust God in order to keep myself from going into a tailspin every time someone disagreed.

The point of receiving advice from other people is to gain their wisdom and avoid unnecessary errors. However, it can sometimes have the opposite effect. Asking the wrong people for advice can cause you to receive information that is drenched with their deeply rooted fears, jealousy, regrets, or bitterness. In their mind, they just want to caution you, but it can cause you to doubt and discourage you from doing what God is telling you to do. In addition to this, consider that few people in your circle, if any, know everything about your situation. So the advice that they can give is limited, for the most part. Take that into consideration, also. Don't let the opinions of others weigh so heavily on you that they hold you back from going where you need to go. Change your circle if necessary. Trust God and trust in yourself. Everything else will work out.

Squad Goals

The most important thing to remember is that there absolutely will be supporters. For most of us, the concerns that we have about public opinions of us are not substantiated. Simply having a heart full of love and faithfulness leads you to win the favor of God and man (Proverbs 3:3–4). If your words and actions come from a place of love and are God-led, it opens doors for you. When you walk and speak confidently, people want to be around you. It's refreshing to have that type of positivity around.

Sometimes, you have to start over in life to receive all that God has promised you. You don't have to feel like starting over means that you will always be by yourself. This process doesn't have to be lonely. Become vulnerable with a few people so that you can make those genuine connections with friends or family members. Everyone in your circle should have their own goals. You don't want them all to be focused on you all the time. They should know how to do some things that you don't. They should have connections that you don't. Each person should have different skill set and a unique perspective that is beneficial to the group and can add value to your life. This is not for the sake of mooching off of them, but so the group has potential to grow. It's a beautiful thing to get this type of camaraderie that is not about competing with each other. It's about building each other up, and celebrating a win for one like it's a win for all, because it is. When any one person in the group accomplishes a goal, that not only brings more knowledge to the group, it builds confidence and morale because you all can see that it is possible.

There will always be people that will help you get where you need to go. Keep in mind that they may not be the same people who you have had in your squad up until this point, and that's okay. Be open to new people and influences that God brings into your life to assist you on your journey. In addition to this, focus on making sure that you have one or more mentors in your corner who have your best interest at heart and who push you toward God's plan for you. These are people who you can consult for sound advice if you need a second opinion during a more difficult season. These people will also celebrate your successes with you because they understand what all you had to go through in order to come out on top.

CHAPTER 5

Pray

"And to know this love that surpasses knowledge — that you may be filled to the measure of all the fullness of God."
Ephesians 3:19, NIV

Me, Authentically?

The majority of what we have accomplished stems from the way that we see ourselves. At one point or another, everyone deals with self-esteem, self-worth, and self-image issues. The way we see ourselves gets clearer when we look through the lens of God. However, the only way to look through the lens of God to see what He sees, is to actually be in a relationship with Him. Think of the relationships that you have with your closest friends, your parents, or your grandparents. The only way to develop an intimate relationship with someone new is to spend quality time with them, just as you did with those closest to you. You have to move past the pleasantries and begin to talk about the real issues — the deeply personal things that you usually keep to yourself. You begin to tell them the things that you fear the most as well as your sincerest desires.

After time spent together, you learn what they like and dislike. You begin to understand how they operate as well as how they view the world. And, of course, you learn what they think about you. You can see how much they love you. In their interactions with you and their advice for you, you can tell that they have your best intentions at heart. Spending quality time with God will change your whole life, largely because it changes your perspective. Take advantage of the fact that we have the opportunity to develop a personal relationship with God Almighty. Make time in your day for Him. Our spirits crave a connection with God. We often feel a sense of lack even when on the surface things seem perfect, because physical things cannot fulfill our spiritual needs.

Most of us have heard story after story of people who became successful or have made it rich and then became deeply depressed. In almost every instance, you'll hear someone asking how that person can be so depressed when they have so much wealth and every opportunity in the world. However, in this physical world, it is easy to forget that we have spiritual needs. It is easy to believe that success, wealth, or fame will solve all of our problems. Many hope that by achieving their goals, they will change the way they see themselves. They hope that will be enough to abolish their insecurities. They live with a hope that if millions of people love them, then maybe they will finally feel loved. Unfortunately, this isn't always true because fame is not true love. In the few cases where it may be true that they feel validated and loved because of their success, their happiness is then tethered to the opinions of other people. So if the world decides tomorrow that they aren't as good looking or talented as another individual and choose not to support them anymore, their feelings of self-worth are severely damaged. Your success, your money, even your brilliance does not make you who you are. God created you very specifically. He is the best, and only way to see your true self clearly. Your relationship with Him allows you to be yourself authentically, regardless of what other people think.

Psalm 37:4 says, "If you delight yourself in the Lord, then He *will* give you the desires of your heart." I used to love this memory verse as a kid, mostly for selfish reasons. I was happy that I was going to get everything that I wanted! I would think, *I'm basically already a millionaire. Done. What's next on the list?* Of course, as I got older I gained a deeper understanding of the scripture. I got a new perspective. When I would hear the verse, the "delight yourself" part would stick with me. I realized that the relationship with God is the most important part. It's also the most rewarding part. It should be enjoyable to spend time in the presence of God every day, not just a weekly chore for Sunday mornings.

In the Key Word Study Bible, the Hebrew translation for the phrase *delight thyself* comes from ânag, which means "to be soft or pliable." The definition confused me at first because it is so vastly different from what I naturally think of when I hear the term delight. Then, I remembered how in the scriptures, God the Father is referred to as the Potter and the Creator, and we are the clay. We have to be willing to be molded into who we are created to be, *pliable. Desires* comes from the Hebrew word mish'âlâh, which means a *request* or *petition.* This was interesting because I'd always thought of a desire as something that someone just wanted really badly. However, the definition in this sense is a request or petition. This implies that *the want* must be great enough that it is spoken to someone who could change the situation. Simply wanting it isn't enough. You have to ask. Lastly, heart, which is lêb, refers to the *feelings* and is usually used to represent an "*aspect of the immaterial inner self.*" When we become pliable, God can mold us as needed, and then He will give us the petitions we speak that come from the very core of who we are.

That sounds cool, on paper, but you may be wondering why God would have to mold you into anything before giving you what you really want. Most people really don't like the idea that God would want to change them. But, let's change the perspective. God isn't out to get you. He isn't your enemy. He is a loving Father. A good father doesn't just give his children everything that they want when they want it. If he did, they would end up spoiled rotten. He teaches them how to be decent human beings and helps them develop their natural gifts so that they can be successful adults. Along the way, he gives them the things that they desire — phones, cars, etc. — as they are able to handle them. Giving a car to a 12-year-old is not beneficial to her. She's not ready for that type of responsibility, no matter how much she desires it. Being pliable to God simply means that you are willing to trust Him with your present and your future. It means knowing that He will mold you so that you are ready for the desires of our own heart. The things that you want deep in your spirit are things that coincide with His plans for you, that He has placed inside of you. God wants you to be willing to go through the process of maturing, either naturally or spiritually, in order to handle your own desires when you receive them.

We have to remember that God is *for* us. He has the best of intentions for us. By seeking Him and asking for our hearts' desires, we can see His plans fulfilled in our lives.

> *"For every one that asketh receiveth; and he that seeketh findeth; and to him that knocketh it shall be opened."*
> Matthew 7:8, KJV

In this passage in Matthew, Jesus reminds us that God is a loving Father. He states that if humans, who are sinful by nature, will give good gifts to their children, then of course God who is perfect also wants to give His children amazing gifts. We just have to ask. Unfortunately, so many people are raised to believe that things will just happen if it is meant to happen. They believe that what we want the most is at the whim of fate. Maybe it will happen, which would be amazing. But, if it doesn't happen, then it just wasn't meant to be. Still, Jesus says that you have to ask for it. Speak it. Again, your words have power, and God wants you to come with the confidence of a child asking her dad for what she needs. When you know that your father loves you, you shouldn't be afraid to come to him boldly, requesting what you need because you know that it is his responsibility as a provider to give you what you need to survive, and that he wants what is best for you.

Recently, I heard a preacher tell a story about heaven. In the story, an angel was giving Peter a tour of heaven, and they passed a door with Peter's name on it. Peter asked what was inside, but the angel insisted that he didn't want to know and that they should continue with the tour. Peter, being the ballsy disciple that he was, decided to run into the room anyway. When he opened the door, he saw tons of rows of shelves. On each shelf, there were packages with his name on it. Peter asked his guide why there were so many packages in this room labeled with his name. The angel replied that these were all of the blessings that God had set aside for him in his life on earth. So Peter became infuriated, like many of us would have. Peter asked, "Why didn't I get them when I was struggling?" The angel just shrugged and said that he never asked for them. That story struck a chord with me. How many things am I missing out on because I was too busy taking things into my own hands. Why not ask God for what we need out of faith? That is what he is waiting for in order to release unimaginable blessings into our lives. Jesus doesn't just say to ask. He says to seek and to knock. These two commands require that you get your hands dirty. If you aren't seeking, why would you expect it to just appear?

In the STEM program in my college, students were encouraged to get summer internships. Professors would find various programs, and they would post them on a wall in the science building. There was literally an entire wall full of potential internship opportunities. It was easy enough for every STEM major to apply to several programs for many different interests. In spite of having all of the options available, there were still multiple people every summer without an internship. The student could have a perfect GPA and not get an internship simply because they didn't apply. They didn't look through all of the given options or even search for programs that focused more specifically on their academic or professional interests. Maybe they couldn't decide which program to apply to, or maybe they wanted a specific internship but put it off too long. Either way, they didn't want it enough to put in the work required to find one and get accepted. Wanting it simply isn't enough. It's not going to fall in your lap. Will you put in the work to find a way to make it happen, instead of just making excuses as to why it won't? The most significant opportunities that you receive are things that you actively go after. The relationships, experiences, and material possessions that mean the most to you are the ones that require the most effort to get, keep, or earn. It can absolutely be within your ability to obtain, but it can be lost because there was a lack of effort. Don't miss out on receiving God's best for you because you won't take any chances or put in any work.

If you have ever watched a crime drama, then you should be familiar with this process. In these shows, the detectives see a crime. They start asking questions to every person who is relevant to the case either by being associated with the victim or the suspect. Once they have information they use it to begin searching for physical evidence. They search the crime scene for fingerprints and other forms of DNA. They analyze the blood splatter and the broken glass until they have enough information to arrest the suspect or at least obtain a search warrant from the court. When the police officers get to the suspect's home, they knock on the door hard with authority. They bang loudly so that any person in the house, whether they are in the shower or sleeping, can hear the knock and open the door. The power with which they knock comes from the authority that they have from the city and the added protection of a court order signed by a judge. They now have a right to be there because they have a warrant to *search* for illegal drugs, weapons, or even kidnapped people.

We have the same authority over our circumstances. If you are knocking and the door hasn't opened, knock harder. It has already been decreed that it must open. Use your God-given authority to gain access to those opportunities. Create an opportunity. Change the narrative in your mind regarding what you are able to do. If police officers knocked timidly, many people wouldn't open the door. This is mainly because the occupants would not be able to hear the knock, but also because they wouldn't respect the authority of the officer. The timid knock is like asking the suspect if they mind allowing their police unit to search the property, you know, if it's not too inconvenient. *They can just come back later if it's too much of a bother at the moment.* A powerful knock indicates that the officers are coming in one way or another; it would behoove the occupant to open the door unless they want it to be broken in. When you realize the authority that you have, your actions change to reflect that authority. Walk with that certainty through every situation in your life.

Consistently spend time with God in your daily life. Allow yourself to develop a real relationship with Him and learn just how important and valuable you are to Him. Seeing yourself the way that God sees you and recognizing your worth is the only way to realize your full potential in this life. It gives you the confidence to speak up for yourself and ask for what is rightfully yours as promised in His word. Living authentically allows you to the freedom to pursue your dreams in spite of any obstacles that may arise. Allowing yourself to be molded by God into the woman you are called to become gives you the opportunity to be even greater than you ever imagined.

Intentional

"Cultivate these things. Immerse yourself in them. The people will all see you mature right before their eyes! Keep a firm grasp on both your character and your teaching. Don't be diverted. Just keep at it. Both you and those who hear you will experience salvation."

1 TIMOTHY 4:15 – 16, MSG

CHAPTER 6

How Bad Do You Want It?

In any athletic sport, a good coach will motivate you to put in the work. Greatness comes from a combination of natural ability and the commitment to study and develop your craft. No matter how much natural ability you have, it is absolutely imperative that you dedicate a specific amount of time to not only maintaining your ability, but pushing yourself to get better. When you are training, you get to a point when you meet your maximum weight limit, the fastest speed, or farthest distance; whatever the case may be for the specific sport. It is at that point when a good coach will try to motivate you to do just a bit more. They are not trying to injure you; they want you to shatter that glass ceiling in the mind that is saying that this is all that can be done. The limitations are in your head. You don't start to grow until the process gets challenging.

However, you won't even get to this point without making the decision to intentionally dedicate time to practice, study, and develop every day of every week. This sounds pretty extreme in our "everything in moderation" type of world, but you can't radically change your circumstances in one hour a week intervals. There comes a point that you have to decide whether or not you are going to be all in. Are you desperate to fulfill God's will in your life? Olympic athletes don't only work out for thirty minutes, three days a week. I highly doubt they have ice cream for dessert every night. That's not how they go about achieving their personal best. It takes a lot of effort. More than likely, it's much more than you are accustomed to doing. It takes giving up some things that you like for what you want the most. It will take everything that you have. It will challenge your existing thoughts, beliefs, and habits. Yet, the rewards that come from succeeding will be far greater than anything that you ever gave up. Even though it will feel like a huge sacrifice in the beginning, after you have succeeded, you will be so astounded by your accomplishments that you won't miss the things that you sacrificed at all. You may even wish that you would have given them up sooner now that you know how nice the other side of the struggle looks.

In order to get a sense of the urgency of the situation, think of a video clip that you have seen of a lioness hunting a gazelle. Once the gazelle realizes that the lioness is nearby, it runs full speed away from the area. It doesn't continue drinking water or just walk away. It runs as fast as it can. It changes directions if the lioness gets too close, but it keeps going until it has completely escaped; otherwise, it's as good as dead. The death may be immediate, but many times it is a slow death of the lions tearing and eating bits of its flesh at a time. It is horrible to think about, but the bible refers to the devil as a lion "seeking whom he may devour" (1 Peter 5:8 KJV). It also informs us that he comes "to steal, and to kill, and to destroy" (John 10:10 KJV). And, it's not just your life that he wants.

The devil wants to steal your dreams and your future. He is on the hunt, and he would love nothing more than to leave you unaccomplished and hopeless, spending the rest of your life bitter and full of regret as your spirit dies more and more each day. As much as we would like to casually make gradual changes, it doesn't work like that. You will never reach your full potential if you don't fight for your life. Don't get me wrong, it is not a matter of being scared of the enemy. The victory is yours. Christ has already won that through His resurrection. The only caveat to all of this is that you have to get in the fight. Deciding not to participate is deciding to lose a fixed fight. It is not until you decide that you are going to take God at His word, and give it all that you got, that you will be victorious. This is your one life and your one opportunity to see God's plan for you come to fruition. You'll never regret trying too hard to achieve your dreams. Decide that you are going to claim the promises of God for your life. Be intentional in your efforts. Commit to the process, and you will be amazed at the results.

Limiting beliefs

Whatever you believe to be true will determine your reality in this world. Those beliefs change the way you think and the decisions you make for the future. Do you trust God to carry you if you take the leap of faith? Do you think that you can accomplish your goals in spite of your past and regardless of your current struggles? Most people hope that they will accomplish their goals, but they don't necessarily have faith. They don't put all of their effort into those goals because they don't want to be disappointed. Then, they end up not being successful because they didn't put all of their effort into the achievement. Lacking faith can cause working toward a goal to become an extremely destructive cycle.

If a woman is attempting to lose a significant amount of weight in order to regain her optimal health, it will take a complete lifestyle change for those changes to become permanent. She will be able to eat healthy and work out for a few days or even a few months off of sheer willpower. However, at some point she will be tested.

Whether it is a stressful day or a celebration, she will be tempted to return to her bad habits. If she has not changed her core beliefs about health and hasn't committed to a lifestyle change, the one piece of cake at a birthday party can turn into a whole week of eating large portions of all the junk food that she felt like she'd been missing out on, with no vegetables in sight. On the contrary, if her perspective on food and health has changed, she can eat the piece of cake in celebration, and then return to her new way of eating. She may even choose to skip the cake altogether. In the long run, actions will follow the core beliefs. Without changing your thoughts and the things that you believe, it will be impossible to make permanent changes necessary to excel.

Modesty

Another way that limiting beliefs manifest in good girls is through modesty. Many good girls have this false sense of modesty engrained into them from a very young age. On dictionary.com, modesty is defined as "freedom from vanity, boastfulness, etc." The translation from the Greek in the Key Word Study Bible states that modest comes from the word *kosmios*, which means "orderly" and "of good behavior." More synonyms would include *reverent*, *acting in a way befitting holiness*, and *honorable*. This has seemingly morphed into the understanding that we are never allowed to say nice things about ourselves or else it is considered to be self-righteous or proud. It is okay to love yourself and be confident in the person God created you to be, and it is okay to say it out loud. There is a difference between believing that we are not better than anybody else and believing that we are not worth anything. How can it please God that not only are you not confident in who you are, but you actively speak against yourself? You are made in the image and likeness of God. That alone should keep you from believing certain things about His creation.

Really think about it for a minute. Why not you? Why are you ashamed of what you have to offer? After Adam and Eve ate of the tree of the knowledge of good and evil, our all-knowing God went into the garden and still wanted to commune with them. And they hid themselves because they were naked. It almost seems comical. They had always been naked, and it had never been a problem before this point. God gave them everything that they needed when He created them, but after they believed the lie of the serpent and ate of the fruit, they became too ashamed to present themselves before God. Suddenly, they felt insufficient, and this is how so many of us are living our lives. God was very specific when He created you. He knows everything about you. Yet, now you feel like what you have is not worth presenting to the world or worth giving back to Him. You are believing a lie. He knows what you have, and He has said that you are enough. He has chosen you to be a part of His plans. Your true potential is not dependent on your feelings. However, your feelings have an impact on how much of your potential will be realized. God has given so much to you. What are you doing with it? Are you just hiding away your gifts and talents? Are you still afraid that what you have isn't good enough?

Even after Adam and Eve sinned and hid themselves from God, He was still loving enough to make them some clothing so they would not feel vulnerable in their nakedness. He didn't just wash His hands of them and leave them to their own devices. The things that you feel most vulnerable about have a purpose in your life. God will give you confidence to be able to continue boldly in spite of your perceived inadequacies. However, eventually you have to change what you believe. At the end of the day, your beliefs determine how far you are able to go in life. You can't accomplish the most challenging dreams if you don't even believe in yourself. Your mind won't naturally attempt to do something that it has determined is impossible and not worth the energy expenditure. Expand your mind. Open yourself up to the opportunities that you'd previously said could not be done. Trust God with your life because He literally has you covered all of the time. Change the way you speak about yourself. See what He sees. It will really change your whole life.

Declarations

> *"For by your words you will be justified,*
> *and by your words you will be condemned."*
> Matthew 12:37, KJV

What kinds of things are you saying to yourself? Think about the common phrases that we use to explain our emotions or situations.

There's no way in the world. I wouldn't be caught dead doing that. Ugh, you're killing me. I can't take it anymore. LOL, I'm dead. I'm too through with you. There's no way that I can afford that. I quit. I can't do this. It's too expensive. Kill me now. It probably won't happen, but… I'm so broke right now. The struggle is real.

These are a few of the expressions that I hear people say every day just about everywhere I go. You'll hear them on TV and see them posted all over social media. When you talk about who you are and what you are capable of doing, are you speaking life? Just like your beliefs, the words that you say have a direct impact on your future. "Life and death are in the power of the tongue," (Proverbs 18:21a, KJV). God gave us authority over every situation. That authority means that the situation has to succumb to our words. The things we say create change, whether it is positive or negative. Ensure that the words you choose speak life and faith into your situation.

I am guilty of making statements that are full of fear, doubt, and anxiety. We all are. For some reason, it seems to come more naturally for us to say the negative things about ourselves and our dreams than it does for us to speak positivity. It is as if actually daring to say the words that we want to hear out loud will jinx you, causing it to never happen in real life. Despite the way this sentiment feels, it couldn't be farther from the truth. Your feelings are not factual. That whole perspective is rooted in fear. Say the good and stop giving the fear of the bad so much power. Speaking it gives your mind the permission to explore how it *can* be done.

There is power in the spoken word. We all know this. This isn't a new concept by any means. Words can hurt, and they are eternal. Once you have made a hurtful statement, it's nearly impossible to take the sting out of them, and it's absolutely impossible to take back what you said. The seed has been planted. People's perception of you, the situation, and even of themselves can be changed by that one comment. That's why there are certain things we wouldn't dare say to little kids. We don't want to plant seeds of doubt in them or say anything to affect their sense of self-worth. It can easily take years for someone who has been verbally abused to regain confidence and begin to believe positive things about themselves. Unfortunately, at some point we forget how impactful words really are, especially when we speak about ourselves. The insecurities and doubt that we feel begins to take precedence in our speech, to our detriment.

However, words can also heal and create life. You have the ability to change someone's whole day with just your words. You are able to say something that completely changes a person's perspective on a topic. Words give you the ability to communicate your deepest feelings and create lifelong connections with other people. They can give a person the confidence to continue to press past any adversity that may arise. They are more significant than we think. We have to be intentional with our choice of words. We must make an effort to ensure that the things that we say promote the reality that we wish to see in our lives as well as in the lives of those around us.

As children of God, we are supposed to speak things into existence. The Bible is literally full of laws for our lives that we just have to believe and declare to activate. Even if you don't believe it at first, speak them anyway. We are called to speak "those things which be not as though they were." (Romans 4:17) Declaring the truth of God is an act of faith in itself. This is because "faith cometh by hearing, and hearing by the word of God." (Romans 10:17) We hear the word of God by declaring it over our lives, and in doing so, faith is produced. When we really know the promises of God and believe them as fact, our perspective shifts. When our perspective shifts, our actions follow. Pay attention when you are communicating. Start by simply being aware of what you are saying. When you respond to people's questions about yourself, what kinds of words do you use? Is it harsh and bitter or full of doubt? Once you start listening, you won't be able to stop. You'll catch yourself speaking negativity, and you will hear others say it about themselves. It will be like daggers in your ears. It's almost overwhelming at first. Then, it will be easy to choose your words more wisely and speak the truth over your life.

In addition to changing your speech in casual conversations, intentionally formulate some biblically based declarations that you can decree over your life every morning and every evening. The goal is to bombard yourself with truths that directly counter the lies that you have allowed to run rampant in your mind for years. You want to hear them so much that when people speak against you or try to project their fears onto you, you won't believe it. In fact, you want to be so full of God's word that you will actually tell people that they have to change the way they speak around you, especially when it comes to how they speak about you.

When you create them, work based off of your honest, current feelings. Find scriptures that address those negative feelings, and write them somewhere that you see regularly. If you lack confidence, read Philippians 4:13. If you feel hopeless, read Psalm 16:8–9. Do some digging, and you will be surprised by how much you can relate to the sentiments expressed throughout the Bible. Post them on your walls or mirrors. Declaring them to yourself will feel silly when you first start, but keep saying them. It only feels that way because in your heart you don't believe it yet. Say them five times in a row if you need to do so. Plant those seeds, and you will see that after a month, it will be so much easier to proclaim. Not only will you be able to say them easily, you will see changes in your life in those areas.

Here are a few bible-based declarations to get you started:

I have everything that I need. *Philippians 4:19*

I am a daughter of the Most High God. *Romans 8:16*

I have dominion over my situation. *Psalm 8:6*

God's promises are true and they apply to my life. *Deuteronomy 7:9*

I walk with confidence because God is with me. *Deuteronomy 31:6*

Let Your perfect will manifest in my life. *Matthew 6:10*

And my best is yet to come. *1 Corinthians 2:9*

Stretching Hurts!

At the beginning of the year, I began doing stretches as a part of my morning and evening routines. This was a way to force myself to be more intentional in my day rather than just waking up at the last minute and falling out exhausted at the end of the night. One day when I was stretching, I actually realized that I was cheating! In some parts of my body, the pull from the stretch was a welcome relief from the built up tension, but in others, it was painful reminder of how much flexibility I'd lost over the years. In those more uncomfortable stretches, I would only stay for a second or two because I didn't want to feel the discomfort. However, from my gymnastics and dance classes years ago, I know you are supposed to hold the position for much longer — like at least thirty seconds or even up to a minute or two. By holding the position, it forces your body to adapt and grow to this new level. That's what helps you become more flexible. However, my natural reaction to being stretched was to pull back and return to where I was comfortable so I could to avoid the pain. I think that's true for most people. In life, far too many of us shy away from anything that makes us uncomfortable. We all want to have an easy, problem-free life. Therefore, most people won't apply for a job that seems like it is beyond our capabilities. We don't try new things if we aren't confident that we will excel. However, if you are completely comfortable, you're likely not growing at all.

Of course, it's easy for us to think about making intentional changes for our lives. Who doesn't want to live the life that God has for them? Yes, we want what's best for ourselves, but there is an equal an opposing desire that we have. And, that is the desire to remain the same. We just want our situation to change. We probably even want some of the people around us to change. But, it can be so hard to look in the mirror and say, "*I'm the one that needs to change.*" It's challenging to look at your flaws and what you are doing that prevents you from reaching your next level. In addition, overcoming your own weaknesses is a daily battle that most aren't consistent enough to actually overcome. After that realization, I made more of an intentional effort to hold through the stretching. I did so because if you press through the pain and discomfort for long enough, it will no longer be painful. Your body adapts and you will be stronger. You'll be able to go even farther than before, and the excitement of getting better allows you to welcome any pain or resistance that comes with the next level challenges. In the end, the freedom and ease that comes with the added mobility is worth so much more than the uncomfortable and sometimes painful process it takes to get there. So stretch yourself; you won't regret it.

CHAPTER 7

Lack

"Who provides food for the raven when its young cry out
to God and wander about for lack of food?"

Job 38:41, NIV

We hate being in a situation where we don't have enough of
the things that we need. Wondering how we will get enough
or when help will arrive makes us uncomfortable because we
want everything to be perfect. It makes us feel like we are out of
control of our own lives. Deep down, all most of us want is to be
comfortable. We don't want to be unhappy or inconvenienced in
any way. We want what we want, and we want it to be easy to get
when we go for it. However, I'd argue that for the majority of us,
lack is what we need the most.

If nothing is missing, people become complacent. And,
unfortunately, complacency is where dreams go to die. We obtain
a few things in our lives, and we think our work is done. Degree,
check. Steady job, check. Got a furnished apartment and cable,
check. Church is great, so we're good to go. It becomes easy to
get into a routine of doing the same old things, every single day.

Life is easy for the most part. It seems like there's nothing more to do except get married — whenever he comes. We feel like the work is done because we have enough of most of the things that we want. It becomes all too easy to forget that there is more to be done. We should always be working toward the next step. There is always a bigger dream and a larger challenge for us to overcome in order to better ourselves naturally and to grow spiritually. God always has unfathomably huge plans for our lives, and this is the best time to work toward them. We have the time and energy, but too many of us are wasting it because we are so complacent. Life is too comfortable.

We know that necessity breeds invention, and it is absolutely true. But, not many people want to be low enough to ever get to the place mentally, emotionally, and especially not financially, to where your default nature kicks into gear — the place where you are past the point of just being frustrated about the situation. You are past the point of rationalizing why it can't work, because you know that something has to work. It *must* work. We forget that we are made in the likeness of God, the Creator of the whole universe. Like Him, we have the ability to create. We have the ability to completely change our circumstances because we are children of the Most High God. Some people know that innately. It is easy for them to push past seemingly insurmountable obstacles in order to succeed. And, we look at them in awe because we don't understand how they did it, and also because we don't realize that we are capable of doing the same things.

This is not to say that we should live in poverty or that God doesn't want us to have nice things, because that would be untrue. God wants us to be successful in life. Jesus literally said, "I am come that they might have life, and that they might have it more abundantly." (John 10:10b, KJV) Understand that being complacent is not the same as living abundantly. Being comfortable is not the same as being successful. Success requires work. It involves putting consistent effort into the things that will turn dreams into reality. It means sacrificing your free time, favorite shows, and some nights with friends in the short term so that you can see the long term benefits of true success. Living abundantly is having more than you need and more than you expected. The lack is simply a driving force to get you started and to keep you going. It is a reminder of both what is missing currently as well as what could be one day in the future. Instead of focusing on what is missing, *make* it what it could be.

Look for the opportunities within the lack. In the area in your life that increasingly bothers you because you need or want more, you'll find your opportunity to do something that has never been seen before. Too often we want our opportunity to come wrapped in a box with the shiniest wrapping paper and the perfect bow. We want someone to walk up to us and tell us, "Hey this is your opportunity! Take it now!" However, by the time the opportunity is in plain sight, everyone else will see it and will also be going after it. Once everyone is doing it, it's probably too late. The best results come from seeing the need and being the first to offer a solution or being able to revolutionize what is being done currently. For instance, have you ever seen an *As Seen On TV* commercial for something and thought, *I could've made that.* Maybe you have heard an older friend or relative talk about a product or service that was on the market that they just knew would be big, and they should have jumped on it in the beginning. Yet, they didn't, and it was a missed opportunity. This constantly happens to far too many people, whether networking for a new job before the application process officially starts or learning a new language because we have a goal of visiting a specific country one day. Most of us won't even buy a replacement umbrella that we know we need because we don't expect it to rain soon and end up running through the rain to a store to purchase one the next time rain does come.

In essence, make the most of your season of lack. They say necessity breeds invention. Get creative. If you're lacking in your career, find networking opportunities. You can even start by just building better relationships with your coworkers and management so people will think of you as things come up. If you're lacking financially, try picking up a second job or start a side business selling things to friends and neighbors until it can grow even bigger. Sell your products online through existing platforms to make beginning much easier. Whatever you lack in your life is an opportunity for you to challenge yourself to grow — to do what it takes to crawl out of that pit. In the end, it will show you what you're really made of, whether you'll wallow in it or overcome.

However, you'll notice that even once you have gotten to the place where you feel that you can relax, after a while of being comfortable, you will begin feeling the lack again in another area. By nature, we always want more. Knowing that God "is able to do exceedingly, abundantly above all that we ask or think, according to the power that worketh in us," makes it natural for us to push for greater in every area of our lives (Ephesians 3:20, KJV). Again, this works out perfectly for us because there's always more work to be done. When self-made millionaires reach that status, they don't just stop at that point. Even if their goal was solely to be a millionaire, becoming one is not the end of the game for them. This is partially because they want to remain millionaires, which requires insight and intentionality, but they also still have the desire to create. They still have more ideas to try and more opportunities to take advantage of in life. This cycle is what drives us to our fullest potential instead of settling for comfortable.

Be mindful that this is not only for material gain. God wants us to be actively searching for a deeper relationship with Him. Through this relationship, He will begin to reveal not only things that will make your life better, but also ways that you can help other people. Your increase is not just for you; it is so God can be glorified through your life. The lack can show you what you need, but it also can show you how resolving it can solve larger societal issues. God can use you to be a catalyst for change in your family, school, community, or the whole world if you are willing to allow yourself to be used. Look at the advancements in technology that stemmed from the need to interact with people more quickly regardless of the physical distance that separated them. Handwritten letters that were transported by mail carriers on horses weren't good enough. So telegraphs emerged, and then telephones followed. Now, there are more instantaneous ways to send text, picture, and video messages than I can easily count. People can be in two completely different countries and still have a face to face conversation. Our whole culture has changed simply from one need to connect.

It seems like everybody talks about how you can change the world if you just put your mind to it. But, seriously, it's true. In science, it's called the butterfly effect when small changes have enormous impacts. We hear it all the time when some company makes it big or some person invents a new product. One of the main questions that the interviewer asks is, *"Did you ever think it would get this big?"* The answer is often no. The inventors were just doing what they needed to do at that moment. Then, as they worked on it, other people realized that they needed that product or service as well.

I imagine that the creator of Spanx just wanted a smoother fit for her dresses. After creating it, she realized other people may need this, too. Now, millions of women worldwide have bought Spanx products to have a better overall appearance in their outfits. This major multimillion dollar empire all came from one woman creating a resolution for a lack in her life. A lack, mind you, that most people would deem too insignificant to even try to fix. However, because she decided to do something about it, the owner now has millions of dollars to work on new ideas and try even more things. Putting in the work in one area created an abundance that now gives her the ability to do so much more.

What's even more amazing is that the children of God have an advantage. The God effect. God is able to do the impossible when we start aligning our lives with His promises. Unfortunately, way too many Christians are complacent. They see lack as a nuisance to be prayed away so that they can get back to being comfortable. Instead, use the lack as motivation to *do* something. Be faithful and consistent with doing the things that you are able to do yourself. Put in your best and receive God's best for you, which is far better than you could imagine.

Push

After college, I constantly said that I just wanted to be comfortable. I'd stop trying to be rich and would settle for anything better than only having twenty dollars left after all of the bills were paid. Making enough money to pay bills, pay off debt, all while trying to save some money and spend some time actually enjoying life was a struggle. All I wanted was to feel like I was successfully adulting. I didn't want to work hard and stress all of the time. I just wanted to make enough money to chill. Then, one day after Bible study, I was watching a medical drama on TV. On the show, there was a major emergency that brought in dozens of patients, overcrowding the emergency room. A particular patient had such severe injuries the doctors stopped attempting to provide medical care and just gave him ice chips and blankets in an effort to make him comfortable. Suddenly, I realized that I had never heard them talk about being comfortable before.

The doctors and nurses always wanted the patients to fight for the best quality of life. This could mean that the doctors would suggest intensive surgeries, painful physical therapy, or nauseating medications with potentially devastating side effects, all so that they could have the benefit of fully functioning body parts in the long run. Comfort was only mentioned when there was nothing else that could be done. Comfort was to ease the patient into death. At that moment, I had a revelation that my struggle was intentional. I wasn't comfortable, and it seemed impossible for me to get comfortable for a reason. That's not the stage of life that I am in. It's not the stage of life that you are in! In your twenties and thirties, you have more knowledge, grit, and strength than ever before in your life. Furthermore, you have more energy, free time, and flexibility than you will in the future. This is the time to fight for the destiny that God has set aside for you.

Women who are pregnant will typically carry their baby for about nine months. The baby can only grow so much inside of the pregnant mother before it starts to endanger not only the baby's life, but the mother's also. When the mother gets to the end of the pregnancy, she starts feeling very intense and painful contractions. Although these contractions are uncomfortable, to say the least, they serve as a clear sign that the baby is preparing to get into position to be born. Unfortunately, the baby doesn't come out immediately after the contractions begin. The mom can have contractions for hours, even days before the baby comes. Why doesn't the baby just come out? The baby is completely developed, so what is the hold up? Well, the pain and discomfort of the contractions serve as clear, unavoidable signs to the mother that it is time to get prepared to birth this child. It gives the mother time to get to a place where the baby can be delivered safely. If the baby came with little or no contractions, it could be disastrous. So, in spite of the pain and discomfort that they cause, the contractions continue because the baby must be born in order to experience the promise.

The discomfort that you feel, the angst, the struggle, is all there to tell you that it is time to get ready. You don't have the luxury of casually deciding when you'll begin. When you are pregnant with a purpose, there comes a point when everything starts to shift. And, that baby is coming whether or not you feel prepared. Fighting against it will only cause you frustration. It is informing you that it is time, not asking. Things are lining up, and you have to be in position so that you can deliver because the alternative will be disastrous to your destiny. Similarly, when it is time to push, you have to push. As much as it may hurt you, you have to keep pushing. The baby cannot make it out alone. Although God has a plan for you, you have the choice as to whether that is the life that you want to pursue. However, if you don't prepare and you don't push when prompted, you may not ever be able to experience all that God had in store for your life.

Of course this doesn't mean that you are destined to struggle all throughout this phase of life. The way that you overcome the struggle is to get out of your head and put forth the effort to make all of the dreams into realities. It was a struggle for me, because I was afraid to believe that I could succeed at my dreams. I didn't want to put the work in and then fail. However, the incredible thing is that when you work in purpose, the struggle doesn't seem so bad. There is a satisfaction in grinding, pushing past the fears, and making things happen. It isn't frustrating because there is a reason behind it. The slight glimmer of hope that you see in the beginning becomes this beacon that will draw you in, encouraging you to do even more, work even harder, and encouraging you to push. Your mindset and perspective completely change. Then, as time passes, you are more and more accomplished. The successes build on each other and become something bigger than what you could have ever imagined. As much as we'd all love for it to be otherwise, this only comes with dedication and consistency. This is the life that you have. There will never be a better time to start. On the other side is the birth of the dream and the fulfillment of the promise, but you'll never see it come to fruition if you don't push.

Shake it Up

Every week seems like déjà vu. It is predictable from work to church to school. It's the same friends, same hangouts, and watch the same mind numbing television shows day in and day out. As the next month approaches, we are exasperated by how quickly the month went by and how little we have accomplished. This happens every single month! Well, now it's time to break up the routine. The reason we don't accomplish much of anything from week to week is because we are creatures of habit. Repeating the same actions every week yield the same lackluster results. Every week, month, and year will be the same until you *make* it different. Turn off the TV. Take a day trip out of town. Meet new people. It is the habit of mediocrity that must be shattered. Comfort can cause complacency. Each day, make an attempt to do something different from what you would normally do.

In order to get to the next level, you have to change your thought pattern. The habits that you currently have were created out of the feelings of inadequacies, doubt, and fear of the future. They were made as the result of stuffing your days full of so many favors to help others that you are too exhausted to do work for yourself. They were made from your previous inability to prioritize your needs. The comfort of the norm is crippling your ability to achieve greatness. Unless your norm includes grinding and bettering yourself, it is not a norm that you can afford to keep intact. You are always building your future. Every decision that you make has a role in the future that you will see, whether that future is one that you will love depends on your choices today.

First Samuel begins with the story of Hannah. Hannah was one of two wives of a man Elkanah in the old testament. Even though her husband loved her, she was in despair because she could not give him a child. The fact that Peninnah, the other wife, had multiple children infuriated her. Every year that they would go to make their sacrifices to God, served as another reminder that what she wanted the most hadn't happened yet. One year, after the sacrifices, she did something different. She went to the temple and prayed uncontrollably, fervently. Her prayers were silent, but still so strong that the priest Eli thought that she was drunk. She promised God that if she could simply have a son, she would give him to be raised as a servant in the house of God. She just wanted to be able to *have* the baby. God answered her prayers, and she had a baby the following year.

Once the baby was able to eat solid foods, she fulfilled her promise and gave the baby boy to Eli so he would be raised in God's house. God honored the fact that she kept her promise to Him, and He blessed her with five more children (1 Samuel 2:21). After years of barrenness, Hannah was able to birth not just one child, but six because she was bold enough to break her patterns and petition God for what she truly wanted in life. When He provided what she'd asked, she actually followed through with the things that she promised to do in return. What's more is that the child that she prayed for and gave to Eli to raise, turned out to be one of the most influential leaders of the children of Israel. Samuel heard directly from God and served as a judge for the people. He later went on to appoint the first king as well as his successor. This was all from one woman daring to do something out of the ordinary to receive the gift that she wanted the most.

Greatness demands intentionality. It requires you to try new things consistently, and risks are mandatory. Comfort is the enemy of success. You have to be bold enough to do things that others will not do. Every person has the potential to be immeasurably successful. Success looks different for every person, of course. It is according to the individual's personal desires and God's plans for their life. Sadly, few fulfill everything that they can because the familiarity of the norm is very comforting. Don't fall victim to it! Changing your habits forces you to actually think about what needs to be done. Think about if an old friend called to say that she is coming to your city for the weekend. While you may only meet up for lunch one day, you likely have to rearrange several different things that you had planned to do which changes your schedule for multiple days. The original splash creates an unstoppable ripple effect.

CHAPTER 8

Indecisiveness

"A double minded man is unstable in all his ways."

James 1:8, KJV

Getting rid of your indecisive tendencies can be a very difficult habit to break, but it must be done. The words "it doesn't matter to me" used to slide easily out of my mouth before I could even realize it because I had conditioned myself to avoid decisions for so many years. However, both you and the person you're speaking to will end up angry and frustrated very often if this isn't checked. When I was a kid, my family would go on road trips pretty regularly. I can remember my dad asking us where we wanted to eat. We'd usually say, "It doesn't matter," or "I don't have a taste for anything." My dad would get so frustrated by this. However, at the time and, sadly, for years thereafter, I thought it was being considerate. Sometimes I didn't have a preference for any particular thing so I thought that by not offering, a suggestion I was freeing them to make the decision that best suited their desires. However, for most people it has the opposite effect. It burdens them with the responsibility of deciding what you want, for you.

More times than I can remember, I have been out with friends and at least one or more people were really hungry, borderline hangry. Yet it still took over an hour to make a decision on what to eat, while driving by restaurants! The conversations go from light-hearted to snippy to downright irritable until someone snaps, "I don't care where we go, but I need to eat something now!" Still, they would go without saying where they'd actually like to go. It is sheer insanity. What is worse is if the other person gives a suggestion and the indecisive person starts saying why those suggestions can't work. I know we've all seen the jokes with the exasperated husband or boyfriend trying to figure out what his lady wants to eat. I can't help but shake my head because I know that all too often, it's true. I know I've done that in most of my relationships whether romantic, familial, or with friends. Even with other issues, most times good girls do not recognize indecisiveness as problematic because it is genuinely done with good intentions.

Oftentimes, indecisiveness is the symptom of a deep-seated problem rather than simply not being capable of making decisions. Women are taught not to state their preference because it isn't polite or, for some reason, it isn't socially acceptable to impose their wishes on everyone else. Because of this, even if she knows what she wants or what was best for her, she will wait for the person in charge to make the decision for her. She's made to feel like it's the responsible thing to do, the considerate thing to do, because then the decision would benefit others.

For some women, this tendency comes from a sense of inadequacy and a diminished sense of self-worth. While they may love themselves, they don't believe that their opinions matter to the people around them. If this is the case for you, ask yourself why you feel like your opinion would be burdensome, especially when decisions are small and inconsequential? Why don't you feel like your opinion matters? Presumably, in this situation the people that you are with are ones you actually enjoy, and they are people who love you. If sharing opinions with loved ones is this problematic, imagine how massive the issue becomes when dealing with acquaintances or even strangers.

Of course, the indecisiveness isn't just about the food. It usually affects most, if not all, areas of life. From a young age, good girls get into a pattern of letting people make decisions for them. They become very passive. Since they want to make people happy, they just go along with whatever decision that is made. It keeps life easy. They don't challenge the status quo. As a result, deciding what college to go to, choosing a major, finding a job, negotiating salary, getting into relationships, and keeping friendships all just become things that just happen. But, this cycle must end! You have to be in the driver's seat of your own life if you ever want to succeed at your personal goals. It is very easy to listen to what everyone wants for you and end up in a life that other people think is great for you, but then realize that you are miserable.

Passivity will never create a meaningful and deeply rewarding life. It creates a life of mediocrity. The early bird is getting the worm, and all the others are just hoping it drops a little piece so they don't have to go digging. Passive people operate from the mentality that whatever will be, will be. Everything will align, and it will just happen if it is God's will. Remember that it is definitely God's will for you to accomplish your purpose. However, it is not going to just happen to you. If you want to travel the world, but you never order a passport, then you will never leave the country. The fact that you never left the country doesn't mean that it wasn't meant to happen, it means that you missed your opportunity because you never did the work. Realize that God is for you, but you also have to be for yourself. A passive life is essentially just self-sabotage. Everything that is worth having is worth committing time, energy, and resources toward completing.

Begin to make decisions in your life. If you are going between multiple options, start making a solid decision just as you would if you have two shower gels in your bathroom. Once you get in the shower, you simply pick one. Get comfortable taking control of your life instead of being idle. Become aware of the voice of God, and let Him guide you. Have confidence in the fact that "we know that all things work together for good to them that love God, to them who are the called according to his purpose." (Romans 8:28, KJV) You are completely covered, so there is no reason to stress and worry about every single situation.

Decisions, Decisions

"I call heaven and earth to record this day against you, that I have set before you life and death, blessing and cursing: therefore choose life, that both thou and thy seed may live."

Deuteronomy 30:19, KJV

In every section of this book, there comes a point where I say to make a decision. Decide to speak up for yourself. Choose to live authentically. Decide to believe God's promises for your life. We have so much more control over our situations than we know. Don't overcomplicate things. It is a decision to be committed. It's a choice to be vulnerable. Trusting God is a decision. It really is that simple. Will you or won't you? The more complicated things seem, the less manageable it feels. The mind starts to become overwhelmed by the need to fix everything. Then, it shuts off and decides that it cannot be done, unless you tell it otherwise. Once you decide that it will be done, the mind starts to find a way to make it happen.

When a firm decision is made, things start to get in order because you have power over your situation. Make the call. Provide the definitive answer. I know that it sounds too good to be true. The natural reaction is to retort that it's easier said than done. That may be true in your life if that is what you choose to believe, but the reality is that life doesn't have to be hard and tedious and painful. We don't have to drag ourselves through life hoping that someday someone will do something that will have the positive impact on our lives, somehow. We don't have to waste months and even years of our lives sitting on the sidelines hoping that we will have a chance to play in the game. You're playing the wrong game. You are thinking of life in terms of an organized school sport where the coach only uses the star players for the bulk of the game. Everyone else is just there for when those players get tired or injured.

Instead, think of the last time you played dodge ball. All of the balls are lined up in the middle of the court, and when the whistle is blown, the most fearless people run full speed toward each other to try to get as many balls as possible for their team. Then, the game really begins, and you see how different personalities come out in the game. The people who are most afraid of being hit by the balls are usually the first ones to get hit and become disqualified from continuing to compete in the game. This is largely because their fear causes them to be extremely tense. They are practically attached to the wall or hiding in another player's shadow only to be exposed when they quickly move to dodge a ball. They don't move quick enough because they are overthinking their every move.

Then, you have the players who are a little afraid of being hit by the balls, but they are still excited to play the game. These players won't usually run to the front to get a free ball, but they will run after the available balls in the back of the court and hurl them at opponents. They won't usually try to catch the balls because they aren't sure if they can, and they don't want to get out in the process of trying. Lastly, you have your confident players. They are quick, agile, and able to think on their feet. They aren't afraid to run to the front in the open to get more balls for the team. They dive to catch the balls that were thrown by their opponents. Most importantly, they usually last the longest in the game. Every person has equal opportunity in the game, and while dodge ball is a team sport overall, your longevity in the game is largely dependent on your own confidence, ability, and flexibility. When it all comes down to it and the whistle blows, will you decide to go for it, or will you hide timidly in the background?

The enemy is attacking no matter which path you choose. However, if you go all in, you can fight back and become victorious. Fight for the life that God has set aside for you. Fight so that when you succeed, you can prove to yourself how far you can go when you take God at His word, and put in the work. The main thing stopping you from making the decision is fear. You don't want to be held to those words in case things don't work out. Yet, the fear that is preventing you from making the decision is the same fear that will keep you from committing to the process. When you make the decision, you are cutting the fear off at the head. That decision gets the ball rolling an allows you to think and act differently so that you can succeed. Don't let the fear of the task or the fear of making the wrong decision keep you in a permanent state of paralysis.

Now is the time to go all in. Commit to living an exceptional life. Decide to change your bad habits that are holding you back. Furthermore, for every decision that you make, make a plan for how that decision will play out logistically in your life. Prepare so that when the moment comes that will test your resolve, you already know how to overcome it. Making the decision to change is an act of war against your current self. You have to actively challenge any thoughts and all existing habits to ensure they align with who you need to become. Take on each hurdle one at a time. Focus on what you can do now, and when you can do more, do more. It is not difficult to do, but you have to be intentional and consistent. However, the beauty of the situation is that with each positive decision that you make and each obstacle that you overcome, you are creating new habits — a new normal. These intentional, life changing decisions, will one day become your standard lifestyle that creates an extraordinary life, and that is worth the sacrifice today.

CHAPTER 9

Persistence

Persistence is one area in particular that good girls tend to struggle. Most will go out of their way to give to others and make sure that everyone else is comfortable. Therefore, even asking for something is sometimes difficult. When it involves asking multiple times or continuing to try in spite of the obstacles, we clam up. *Will they be offended that I kept asking after they said no?* To be honest, so many good girls would not even ask for what they needed if someone *inferred* from a previous conversation that they would not be interested. This is because the fight mechanism has been turned off for too long, and there is only flight left. The reality is that you cannot afford to be passive about your dreams. They depend on you to come true. Your future depends on your active response now. Who else can fight for your dreams? No one else even knows the entirety of what they are. You have to hold your ground and commit to doing whatever it takes to give them a chance at survival.

Your dreams are like newborn babies. Everything must be done for them. You may not know exactly what they need at first. Still, it is necessary for you to continue to do the work for them until they mature enough to take care of themselves, or else they will die. It sounds extremely drastic, but that is the reality. That means you do not have the luxury of being passive. It is not all going to be handed to you on a silver platter. Whatever you need, go after it with the fervor of a new mom who is desperate to ensure that her baby survives. Research new ideas. See what people have done in the past and adapt it to what you are able to do right now. When was the last time you took a stand for your dreams and ideas? When will you decide that you will do whatever it takes to push through the complacency, push through the excuses, and do what it takes to get it done? Instead of looking around the room wondering what it could be like, fight for your future! The status quo will not be enough to take you to the next level. It isn't going to drop in your lap.

A Gentile woman approached Jesus because she'd heard of His miracles and wanted Him to cast the devil out of her daughter. Jesus commented in a way that seemed offensive to see how she would respond. If I may paraphrase, He said, *this food is for the children, it wouldn't be right of me to throw it to the dogs* (Mark 7:25–30). What?! Most of us would have walked away offended, hurt, heartbroken, and confused. And we would have missed our blessing. The woman replied, *even the dogs get the crumbs from the table* (28). Then, Jesus granted her request. He liked the fact that she kept her eyes on the prize, which in her case was deliverance for her daughter. She knew that any blessing from Him, even His leftovers, would be enough to change her daughter's course of life.

Will you go for it even if it doesn't come as easily as you thought it would? Will you fight past the hurt feelings to get what you need accomplished? You have to be tough and get thick skin. Destiny is not just a way of life that *happens*. It is something that you achieve after a series of intentional actions. This process may sometimes take several years. However, you must still be intentional about your time. Study your craft and establish detailed steps. Set a timeline to divide this huge vision into manageable tasks. Make small goals every day about tasks that you can accomplish that day, as well as a goal for the week. The only thing that is preventing you from living a life of purpose is yourself. Make the decision and put everything into it.

Discipline

> *"No discipline seems pleasant at the time, but painful. Later on, however, it produces a harvest of righteousness and peace for those who have been trained by it."*
>
> Hebrews 12:11, NIV

It seems like the hardest part about making life changes is, well, just doing it. As soon as you make the decision to go for it, excuses begin to pile up as to why you can't start this week. It is extremely important to set yourself up for success, and that begins in the mind. As a good girl, it becomes habitual to put others first. It is so easy to overrule your plans for other people's needs. Be intentional about your time management. Discipline is a decision, simply put. Create the new habits that will support the life that you would like to create, because the habits that you currently have, got you to the place where you are right now. Major advances only happen after consistent effort is put into creating change.

People may disagree with me and say that discipline is a skill that has to be developed over time. While I understand this point of view, and I used to believe it, I don't believe it anymore. I think as a society we tend to needlessly over complicate things. Exercising discipline *is* a decision. The decision may get easier with time, but the only way you will ever follow through with your commitment is deciding that you will. The only way that you will develop habitual change is by making the decision every day to pursue your goal. You can't be partially disciplined — either you are or you aren't. Regardless of your feelings or mood at the moment, when the time comes, will you go all in or cop out? Are you going to do it or make an excuse? Make the decision to push past your comfort zone every day because the goals that you want to achieve will not be found inside of it.

A hard thing for me to do was stop eating out so much. I would justify eating out because I often work really long days so I'd have to pack two to three meals in order to have enough food for the day. Instead, I wouldn't pack anything, and I would just plan to eat out on those days. It was just easier. However, making those poor decisions wasted a lot of money every week. So maybe I can't prep and bring three meals every day, but I can make oatmeal or grab some fruit in the mornings. I could get quick meals from the grocery store that I could bring that would be cheaper than actually eating out every single day multiple times. At some point, I had to set that boundary even with myself. What can I do to prevent me from eating out so often? How do I prepare so that I can keep this goal?

The best way to go about making these changes is to be specific. Write to-do lists at night for the following day so that you already have a plan of action when you wake up. Schedule reminders throughout the day will keep you on track. Be proactive when challenges arise so they don't become excuses that eventually stall progress. Try not to get complacent with your accomplishments. Take a breather to celebrate your successes, and then keep pushing! You will never regret putting too much effort into accomplishing your dreams. Make a plan, and then make the commitment.

Although being disciplined takes a lot of consistent effort, don't make it a burden. In no time, you will no longer need discipline for that specific task because it will become a habit. Be excited about the new ventures instead of letting it stress you out. It is worth the effort. Walking on the faith of God's promises will lead you to places far better than your dreams! Remember that you are not creating this new life alone. God is with you through every step of the process, because you are putting your trust in *His promises* and fulfilling *His will.*

One Day At A Time

I like to challenge myself. I have had these seemingly crazy ideas that I commit to, then later go on to regret. One December, I jokingly dared my brother not to eat fast food for a year. He refused because he had a busy life and didn't want to commit to something like that. We laughed it off. Then I started thinking about it. Why couldn't I do it? And if there was something that I felt like I *couldn't* do, shouldn't I be challenging it? So I did it. I decided that when the new year began, that I wasn't going to eat from fast food restaurants, mall food courts, or any restaurant with a drive through. I made some clear guidelines so I wouldn't be able to tempt myself or cheat later. Man, did I regret it! At first. When I was going through it, there were so many days when I wanted to rationalize eating fast food. But, I had made a blog to chronicle my year and I didn't want to admit defeat so I kept going. Then, afterward, I was thrilled that I did as well as I did. It was only because of the daily, sometimes hourly decision to keep going that I was able to resist something that was such a big part of my collegiate life.

Likewise, earlier in the year, I watched a documentary on fasting and I thought to myself, I can do that. I didn't want to fast as long as the man in the documentary, but I had been incorporating fasting into my lifestyle and I wanted to do something that challenged me. I only told my brother at the time and he told me to just think about how I'd feel when it was over. See it as completed, and everything else was just a technicality because it was already done. Time just had to catch up to my moment of completion, that was waiting. Perfect! Sounds great. By day three I was over it! Why did I commit to this? I didn't want to do it anymore. I decided that I wasn't going to do it anymore. I told myself that I'd finish day three and be done with it. Literally, I planned the junky foods that I was going to eat for each meal of the next day.

The next morning, all of those feelings were gone. I felt perfectly fine, as I would any other morning. So I went back and forth in my mind as to whether or not I would continue. While contemplating this, my brother texted me. He asked how it was going and reminded me to see the end goal. The timing was unbelievable. It was at that point I made the decision to keep going until the end. I decided no matter what I was going to reach that goal. And once again, I did it! But, I learned so much in the process. Throughout this time, I realized it was too much to think of the whole process at once. I had to think of each day individually. Plan for success today and refuse to worry about how I'd complete tomorrow. That's literally what Jesus tells us to do.

> *"So do not worry about tomorrow. Let tomorrow worry about itself.*
> *Living faithfully is a large enough task for today."*
> Matthew 6:34, The VOICE

This is something that we have all heard, but all too often forget. Live faithfully today, and work on the issues that come up today, but don't bog down your mental space with concerns of the future that may not even be valid next week. It was really great for me to see this in action. During that time I would tell myself that I could do anything for a day. I had done it before so this day would be no different. And it was much easier than thinking about the entire process at once than when I was dreading it the first three days.

Another concept that I had to apply was one Paul speaks of about bringing the body under subjection. He largely used it referring to refraining from sin, but it also applies for living a life of discipline in any capacity. It's mind over matter, simply put. Whether developing work out routines, writing schedules, practice time for your instrument, or morning time to worship, creating good habits require a consistency in your daily disciplines. Each day I had to retrain my thoughts and commit to do what was required in order to press on toward the goal. And this is what will be required for every person who wants to achieve something out of the ordinary. It is easy to remain the same, in practice. You never have to change your thoughts, your behaviors, or your environment. However, if you want something you have never had before and reach new goals, it is going to cost you. If you really believe your goal is worth it, you will make the necessary daily sacrifices of time, sleep, or energy to put toward disciplining yourself in your personal developmental areas.

CHAPTER 10

Just Waiting

"Go to the ant, you sluggard; consider its ways and be wise!
It has no commander, no overseer or ruler, yet it stores its
provisions in summer and gathers its food at harvest."
Proverbs 6:6–8, NIV

If you were to research the lives of ants, you would find tons of information about their very intricate lives within their colonies. Ants can survive in practically any ecosystem in the world and can adapt to any environment. Each ant has a role, and they work together to solve problems and thrive as a community. The ant has no overseer. It instinctively knows what its role is within the colony, and proceeds with what needs to be done. This proverb is a reminder of the importance of being productive. The ants work for their food and even store some away so they'll have some more in case they need it in the future. The scripture goes on to ask, "How long do you plan to lounge *your life away*, you lazy fool? Will you ever get out of bed?" (Proverbs 6:9, The VOICE). Sadly, that is still a valid question thousands of years later.

Many of us grow up with constant supervision in the form

of parents and teachers who give assignments with specific instructions on what needs to be done as well as how to do it. Then, you graduate from school, you leave your parents' house, and you realize with a shock that there is this huge world of opportunity where you have to forge a path of your own. We are so accustomed to being followers that we no longer know how to create a path for ourselves. Instead, we wait endlessly for someone to appear and show us how to go forward. What will it take for you to get up and do what you need to do?

The most common excuse for why people aren't actively working toward any particular goal is that they are waiting for the *right* time to take the *right* opportunity. In the church world, you'll hear people say that they are waiting on God to tell them that it is time to move, or how to move. Girl! You aren't waiting on God; God is waiting on you! Have you done everything that God has already said to do? Probably, not. He's waiting for you to do *something*. Take that leap of faith instead of trying to pray it away. Most people are waiting during a time when they should be making moves. I spent so much time "waiting" for God. I guess I was expecting Him to send archangel Michael personally with a bag of money and detailed instructions on how to reach success without making any mistakes. Years were wasted because I sat around miserable, waiting to be chosen without realizing that God chose me a long time ago.

> *"Before I formed thee in the belly I knew thee; and before thou camest forth out of the womb I sanctified thee, and I ordained thee a prophet unto the nations."*
> Jeremiah 1:5, KJV

Long before we ever desired to fulfill our individual purposes, God had already given us a specific dream and placed a seed for it in our spirits. The seed that is planted, already contains everything that it needs to be successful. It just needs a good environment to grow in, and a gardener who is willing to take the time to tend to its needs. Waiting on God sounds good because it makes people believe that you are doing what you are supposed to be doing in this season. Anyone who wanted to ask for more probably wouldn't because if they continued pushing, it would look like they were trying to steer you away from the will of God. Therefore, saying that you're waiting on God gets them off your case. It sounds like we have done everything possible, and it won't happen unless God intervenes in the situation. But, are you being honest with yourself, or are you using God as an excuse to get out of doing the work? Most people are simply wishing for their dreams to come true like small children wishing on shooting stars. They don't take the time to even research what it will require, much less take steps toward completing the goals.

What exactly are you waiting for God to do? If you are looking for clarity, it comes through action. The reason that you can't see clearly is because you have all of this fear and anxiety clouding your vision. When you begin to work, the fear goes away because you realize the truth, which is that you already have what you need to get started. When that fear is gone, you start to see things as they really are. It's as if there is a boulder in the path that you are walking on, and instead of trying to walk around it or climb over it, you just decided to sit down and beg God to move it. You didn't even try to use the ability God already gave you. If you can't handle this, how can you possibly want more gifts and success from God? You have to show God that He can trust you with more, and you do that by putting to use what you have right now. Everyone has something that they can do in this moment with what they currently have. With every step, you gain momentum and clarity. Don't use God as your excuse to remain complacent.

Focus on what you have instead of what you think you need.

If you don't know what you can do right now, ask God. Do you consistently spend time in prayer and worship? When is the last time that you read the Bible? Many of us say we are waiting for God for answers, but we aren't even communicating with Him. We say a prayer in passing filled with frustration and keep moving without waiting for answers. We aren't even grateful for what has already been done. On the other end of the spectrum, we'll spend twenty minutes whining to God, begging Him to do what He has already promised to do in His Word. Yet, we have no idea how to stand on His promises because we have not taken any time to figure out what they even are and how they apply to our situations. There is always something to be done. Instead of waiting around aimlessly, make the most of the time that you have.

Obedience

"The faith in his heart was made known in his behavior.
In fact, his commitment was perfected by his obedience."
James 2:22, The VOICE

When you feel God leading you to do something, do it. Go with that feeling right then. How many times do you override that feeling, then later go on to regret it? It could be little things like forgetting car keys and having to go back into work to grab them or leaving your kitchen light on all day. It could be something much bigger where your lack of action caused the end of a friendship or relationship. Once we have more information and we realize that we made the wrong call, the first thing is always the immediate thought that we *knew* what should have been done. We are annoyed by the fact that we didn't go with it. God wants to guide us through our daily lives and constantly gives us advice or warnings so that we can avoid some of the pitfalls and have a life of abundance. The problem is that we can't foresee the repercussions of our actions. We think that when we consciously make a decision, we have all of the necessary information. However, God sees what we can't. He knows the thoughts and intentions of the people around us as well as anything that may happen in your life that may bring about an outcome that is different from what you were expecting. Learn to listen to His voice in order to live life without regrets. Follow His voice to live the life of abundance that you are seeking.

Another major point when it comes to being obedient to God is doing what He instructed the way that He instructed you to do it. When God decided to test Abraham, He commanded him to sacrifice his son Isaac as a burnt offering on Mount Moriah (Genesis 22:2). The very next day he got up, packed his things, rounded up his son and some servants, and headed to the place God told him to go. Once he got there, he and Isaac gathered everything that they needed for the sacrifice and began climbing up the mountain. Along the way, Isaac asked Abraham where the animal was that they would be sacrificing. Although Abraham knew what God had assigned him to do, he trusted that God would make a way out of no way. So he told Isaac that God would provide the sacrifice. In the end, it wasn't until Abraham had tied Isaac and was prepared to sacrifice what he loved the most, that the angel stopped him and Abraham noticed the ram caught in the bushes. If he hadn't obeyed God, he wouldn't have been able to prove his love for God; and if he'd been out of position because he went to a mountain in a different city, he would have missed the ram in the bush and killed his son and the promise. Because God is so intentional, there is significance in following the exact guidance.

It isn't just about doing what you are led to do, or doing it how you were led to, the timing is extremely important. We serve an all knowing, all seeing God. He knows what will happen the very next second. Deciding to wait a few weeks in order to schedule that task into your calendar is not good enough. You don't know what opportunities you may have missed in that time. It could be that starting the assignment at that time will allow you to finish it by some point in the future when that idea is needed, or that saying whatever is weighing on your heart will change someone's day. Being at the right place is important, but it only is beneficial if you are there at the right time. It is great to actually complete an application for the job of your dreams. Your résumé can perfectly meet the desired requirements, and you can have excellent references, but if you missed the deadline, you still won't be considered for the opportunity.

It can seem like it's very particular or too constricting, but God is very intentional. Being specific about telling you where the potholes are will help you get to your destination much quicker because you won't be stalled due to sprained ankles or falling flat on your face. GPS would be essentially useless if it only told you the main streets and left you to figure out the smaller turns on your own, or if it told you all of the street names but gave no indication of how far away they are from each other. All of the parts of the instructions work together, and if you skip any of them, the result is usually that it will be longer until you reach your destination. It is essential to your journey to follow the instructions that God gives so that you get to live a life that is more rewarding than anything you've ever dreamed.

Time Is Wasting

"So teach us to number our days,
that we may apply our hearts unto wisdom."
Psalm 90:12, KJV

I mention several times in this book how important it is for you to be intentional about time and time management. This is because I wholeheartedly believe that time is the most valuable asset that you will ever have in life. It is misleading because it is so common. When you are young especially, time feels like an endless supply of moments. However, think of how quickly it goes by. We anxiously await Christmas, starting in October, then a blink later Christmas is over. Before you know it, it is New Year's Eve and you are deciding that this year you will finally achieve a goal so it absolutely WILL NOT be on your resolution list next year. Then, it is March, and you are angry because if you had just stuck with it in January like you said you would, you would have completed your goal already. Can you tell I'm speaking from experience? You get the picture.

Most of us don't really value our time. We theoretically understand that it is limited, but in the moment we often waste minutes and even hours participating in activities that we will likely just forget in a week. We constantly scroll through our timelines on social media throughout the day. We have conversations with people we don't really like about things we don't really care about. Hours are spent watching television programs that aren't in any way applicable or beneficial to real life. What could you be doing instead? Think of all of the things that are sitting on your Life List that could have been completed in the cumulative time spent doing things you will never remember. How could you better spend your time in a way that would make those moments memorable? Maybe studying for a qualifying exam in your industry is less fun than watching marathons of your favorite shows, but passing that test will make you appreciate all of those hours spent preparing for your purpose.

In our society, we have been conditioned to believe that we should only do things that are pleasurable. We should focus our energy and attention on the activities that bring us the most enjoyment. While I do think that life should be enjoyable, I also think that people forget the benefits of delayed gratification. It is perfectly fine to want to watch a show because it is your favorite and you'd like to see how the story evolves. Of course, watching it immediately is the natural preference because it is available at the moment. However, while studying is the least appealing option of the moment, it yields the greatest rewards. Instead of doing what is most fun immediately, use that as an incentive to do what needs to be done. As a result, you get the benefit of completing what you need to do followed by the enjoyment of doing what you actually preferred to do.

Have you ever found out that a celebrity that you like is your age? I legitimately am surprised when I see someone who is my age or younger who is wildly successful by most people's standards. Particularly, I'm referring to ones who have become successful due to marketing their best skills, not those born into wealthy families. I'm not sure if I am more shocked at how much they were able to accomplish in the same number of years on this earth as I have had or by the realization that it actually is possible. When this happens, it reminds me that I can either put in the work for what I really want or just settle for less than my potential by blaming the obstacles that I have experienced. Everyone has the same 24 hours in a day. Make the time. Get it done. Prioritize what you need to do over what you would like to do or what feels good in the moment. Either decide to wake up earlier or stay up later in order to fit more hours of productivity into your day. That is the only way that you will ever see true success in any area of life. Simply saying that you don't have time is a copout. It is an excuse to keep you complacent.

You only have a limited number of seconds on this earth. And, while that set amount of time may equate to hopefully multiple,

multiple decades of life, we will never know in advance how much we have. Meanwhile, it continues to tick away one second at a time with no pauses and most definitely no rewinds! If you make a decision that wastes money, it can cause a setback, but money is replaceable. You are always able to make back what you lost and more. However, putting off taking the necessary steps toward destiny because of laziness, fear, or indecision wastes valuable irreplaceable moments. Use discernment and seek God in your decision-making process, then take action. Make those moments count. Make today count. Once time is spent, it's non-refundable.

Enjoy the Process

> *"A cheerful heart is good medicine,*
> *but a crushed spirit dries up the bones."*
> Proverbs 17:22, NIV

Much of this book so far has been about the work. In essence, you have to put a lot of intentional effort into changing your thought patterns and making permanent lifestyle changes. Don't misunderstand this fact to mean that it has to be hard, tedious, or boring. It is an exciting time when you are able to rediscover yourself. You are able to share your perspective of the world through your gifts and talents. Nothing can compare to the satisfaction that comes from overcoming challenges that you truly believed were insurmountable. I guarantee that you have strengths and abilities that you were not even aware that you had. In discovering them, you begin to love yourself more completely. Enjoy the process, *"For my yoke is easy, and my burden is light."* (Matthew 11:30 KJV) This is an opportunity to live the life that God has for you. Be proud of reaching those milestones. Celebrate the journey.

After you have started to put that intentional effort in

consistently, you'll begin to revel in your emotional, mental, and spiritual emancipation. Burdens of fear and indecision are lifted off of you and you really experience true freedom. Once you get to this point, know that this is where you should have been all along. The people around you may love your new thought processes and actions, or they may not understand it at all. They may even tell you outright that they don't like that you have changed, which is fine. They are free to have their opinions. However, don't apologize for your newfound freedom. Refuse to let any situation or any person have that kind of mentally oppressive hold on you ever again. Live freely and unapologetically. *"For the gifts and calling of God are without repentance."* (Romans 11:29, KJV) The fact that people don't understand you doesn't mean that you are wrong. It may mean that they aren't at the same point on their journey with God. Don't make their confusion cause limitations for you.

Unapologetic

"Stand fast therefore in the liberty wherewith
Christ hath made us free, and be not entangled
again with the yoke of bondage."

GALATIANS 5:1 KJV

CHAPTER 11

Overcoming Fear

"For God hath not given us the spirit of fear;
but of power, and of love, and of a sound mind."

2 Timothy 1:7 KJV

At the core of most of the seemingly valid reasons people give for why they can't choose to live a life of purpose is fear. They fear that doing so means that there is no chance for stability. Everyone thinks of the starving artist who irrationally chooses to have nothing in order to express his or her point of view through their art. They fear that other people will judge their decision to change careers at the age of thirty or move to another city at the spur of the moment. They fear that they will become vulnerable and share their perspective with the world, and no one else will be able to relate to those feelings. It is a natural instinct to have a self-preservation, proceed with caution instinct. However, that instinct doesn't factor in God's ability, because if they are walking in purpose, it is God's desire to bless them because in doing so it brings Him glory.

So how can you overcome the paralyzing fear that prevents

you from even thinking about progressing? Information, of course. Fear typically stems from either the lack of information or misinformation about a given subject. Additionally, the goal may seem completely overwhelming when you think of the big picture. Knowing that you need to start a film company seems daunting when the most you have ever done with videography was create YouTube videos. Take classes on the craft, read about how to create successful business, or work for existing film companies in order to understand what is needed for that type of business. By doing so, you increase your knowledge base and skill level so that when it is time for you to finally take that step into entrepreneurship, you are much more prepared. Every step that you take toward the goal helps to eliminate the fear. And, while there still may be some nervousness at first, completing the tasks that scared you will become the new normal in time. Then, you will be looking for new challenges to conquer.

Another aspect of fear that must be dealt with are those that come from deeply rooted emotional issues. At first thought, you may not believe that there is more to it than the generic nerves and a bit of procrastination. However, think of how long you have wanted to achieve your biggest dreams. How many steps have you taken toward these dreams in the years that you have had them? Why would the thing you want the most be the same thing that you avoid doing the most? Many good girls have past hurt in the form of rejection or physical or emotional abandonment that acts as the underlying reason that causes them to subconsciously reject the thought of creating a situation where she could potentially be publicly criticized for her opinions.

This is the most important part of this section. Do not put your career, business, or goals on hold just because you are afraid. Fear is not a good indicator of whether or not you have a good or profitable idea. If you are doing something new and original, there may always be an element of fear, honestly. It doesn't go away on its own. Going forward with it requires a deep level of vulnerability. You are taking an idea that you have been cultivating for months or even years and offering it to the public. There is no way of telling if people will accept it. However, the voice inside that is causing you to be afraid is just lying to you. If you don't choose to face it head on, it will keep you mediocre forever.

Bold

> *"But without faith it is impossible to please him: for he that cometh to God must believe that he is, and that he is a rewarder of them that diligently seek him."*
>
> Hebrews 11:6 KJV

In 2014, I decided to quit my job and move to from Little Rock, Arkansas where I'd went to college, to Washington, DC. I wasn't fulfilled with my life, and I had to make a decision about what to do next. I didn't have a better job lined up, but I just had to go. Yet, even with the conviction that I had to leave, which was enough to quit my job, I rationalized why it made sense for me to stay in Little Rock a little longer. Primarily, rent was way cheaper. When I told people about my plans, few were supportive. Others literally thought I had lost my mind. But, as soon as I was out there without a safety net, my risk aversive nature just wanted to run back to safety. I even went back to work for the same company for a few more weeks until they found my replacement. To be honest though, the three weeks that I went back solidified my conviction to leave. It was like having a taste of freedom, then voluntarily going back on house arrest. Don't get me wrong, it wasn't that it was a bad job by any means. I enjoyed the people I worked with and the products that I sold, but it just wasn't what

I knew I needed to be doing. It didn't align with the dreams that I had always had. When I moved in September, I sold my car, packed two suitcases and two carryon items, and mailed one box of books. Everything else was left behind, clothes, appliances, the job, and a boyfriend — things that no longer fit me. There was no anger or hurt feelings; I was just getting a fresh start.

At the time, I didn't think what I was doing was bold. It just seemed like a necessary decision. I felt like I needed to follow up on an earlier unrealized plan to move to Washington, D.C. that I'd had right after college. I don't think that we need to just go around doing things that sound bold just to create a confident public façade. Being bold is simply being strong enough to make the decision to follow God's voice and follow His plan for your life. Be confident in your choice to take the less traveled road no matter how it looks to people who are on the outside looking in. For all you know, they may be inspired by seeing you take action.

What is it that you want to do? Who do you want to be? Most importantly, what's stopping you? I know you have heard these questions before, but did you answer them? You should. Get a notebook and list everything that you have a strong desire to do that you have been putting off for years. It shouldn't just be a bucket list full of adventure activities that you'd like to try once. Actually write out career and/or life goals. Maybe you have always wanted to go on a mission trip or move to another country for a year or two. Perhaps, there is a specific industry you would prefer to be working in that you have discouraged yourself from trying because you lack experience on paper. You may want to become debt-free so you can travel the world freely or even become an entrepreneur. Whatever the case may be, spend some time figuring out what those things are, and write them on paper. Write down everything that comes to mind. Then, actually write out what is preventing you from fulfilling them. Have you even made baby steps toward them? Or, is it just an ever-growing list, year to year, of things that you'll absolutely, most definitely do one day? Hopefully, you won't die waiting.

Look at your list again. Look at all of the challenges that you believe are keeping you from reaching your goals. What are you doing to overcome them? Is that you don't have enough money? Have you picked up another job to start saving toward it? Have you stopped splurging on eating out or shopping for unnecessary things so you can save money? If you think that you don't have enough time, you can wake up earlier or stay up later to work toward your goal. Make a schedule to budget your time throughout the day. Is it that you don't know the "right" people? If so, are you placing yourself in situations where you can meet influential people in your field? Are you getting to know the people who are already in your circle so that they will think of you in other conversations in their networks when your skills may be needed? Are you putting in the time developing your skills and building your brand while you're still small, so that when the resources come you can optimize them? Or, are you just waiting for God to remove every single hurdle before you even take the first step?

"For as the body without the spirit is dead,
so faith without works is dead also."
(James 2:26b, KJV)

If you truly believe God for it, you have to do what you are capable of doing in order to make room for God to bless you. God will not provide a Godly husband for you when you won't let go of the trifling boyfriend who you know is not right for you. God won't make you an international make-up guru if you won't go to cosmetology school to study your craft, you don't teach friends and family about make-up, and you barely wear it yourself. You have to put in the work. Make bold choices and move forward with your goals.

CHAPTER 12

Carry Your Bed and Walk

"Then Jesus said to him, "Get up! Pick up your mat and walk."
At once the man was cured; he picked up his mat and walked."
John 5:8–9, NIV

We like to believe that if Jesus were on earth with us today, He would hold our hands through every obstacle that comes in our path. It makes us feel like we are special and being cared for. While God does take care of our every need, the reality is that He is not going to coddle you every step of the way. In order for a baby to learn how to walk, the parents have to stop carrying her. They have to let her discover her own strength by allowing her to support her own bodyweight and balance on her feet. Then, they allow her to find support and stability in the form of walls and coffee tables. Finally, the parents let the baby experiment with taking a step on her own. At any point, if she falls, the mom will pick her back up and balance her on her feet again before allowing her to try learning to walk again.

If you have ever seen a baby learn to walk, you can sometimes see there is fear and frustration in their expressions. At times, they will stand where you placed them and just start crying because they are afraid to fall. Sometimes the baby will stand for a moment, then try to regress back to crawling because she is comfortable crawling. Babies move faster when they are crawling before they learn to walk. They don't understand what's happening; they just want to get to where they are going. However, as the parent you know that crawling is not be a sustainable or practical way of moving around. So even though the baby is uncomfortable and confused, you continue to the process until she successfully masters walking. Similarly, God will place you in situations to encourage you to step out on faith. In the beginning, it feels uncomfortable, and we don't like feeling like we are on our own. We want to go back to our old ways because that makes more sense from our limited point of view. However, God will keep you in that situation until you learn to walk in faith. God does not intend to take every step for you. He wants you to develop spiritually like natural parents want their child to develop physically. He requires you to pick up your own bed and walk.

Jesus was on His way to a religious festival. During his travels, He came across a 38-year-old man who could not walk and had been sitting next to a pool for decades. Seasonally, an angel would stir the water, and the first person to get into the pool would be healed of their ailments. Year after year, he waited for his opportunity to be made whole. What's interesting is that when Jesus asked the man if he wanted to be healed, the man didn't automatically say yes. The man gave a reason why he couldn't be healed. He said that he didn't have anyone to help him get into the pool, and since he couldn't walk, someone always beat him to it. Then, Jesus told him to stand up, pick up his bed, and walk. Only then was the man made whole. (John 5:5 – 9) This man spent decades of his life waiting for the perfect opportunity to arise so that he could get what he wanted the most. Then, when his opportunity came to be healed by Jesus, he was still focused on what he lacked and why he couldn't accomplish what he wanted.

After telling Jesus about his struggles, Jesus didn't placate him to make him feel better. He didn't command anyone to stay with the man and help him the next time the angel stirred the water. He just told him to get up and walk. The man already had everything that he needed, it just needed to be activated. His excuses became irrelevant when Christ told him to get up and walk. *Then* was the man made whole. When Jesus commanded it, all of the other issues in the man's life still looked the same. He had to have faith that if Jesus said for him to do it, he had to be able to do it. The same holds true for you. He wouldn't tell you to do something that you can't do. Understand that after you listen to God's commands, you will be made whole. Whatever it is that you felt was holding you back becomes what you have to stand on. Why are you waiting for life to present you with perfect conditions before you can even walk in your life's purpose? If you trust Him, *do something.* Act in faith. It is not a leap of faith if you can see the next step.

Learning to Fight

"Fight the good fight of the faith! Cling to the eternal life you were called to when you confessed the good confession before witnesses."
1 Timothy 6:12, The VOICE

I heard this analogy once that really stuck with me. Let's say you wake up one particular morning, and you're filthy. Maybe you worked out the night before, then went straight to bed. So you wake up and your stench is so bad it offends you. Your breath smells and tastes bad. Do you stay in bed and pray that God cleanses your body and cleans your teeth, tongue, and gums completely? Do you stay in bed hours or even days begging God to clean you because you still are filthy, and it is getting worse the more you cry out to Him? No, you wouldn't. You are probably grossed out by the thought of it. You would get yourself up, walk to the bathroom, bathe yourself, and brush your teeth. Even if you were literally in the wilderness, you would try to find a river to clean off as much as you possibly could with what was available. Why? It's not because God can't do it. God is able to do anything. It's just that you would not expect God to do it because you know that it is within your power to do it yourself. That is what God requires. He delights in seeing His children walk in the authority that He has already given them. He is not going to drop you into an alternate reality where everything is already done for you because you don't want to do the work.

A major part of the journey is the fight. It is there to develop a strong character in you so that by the time you reach your goals, you know how to handle the success, and you keep your sight on God every step of the way. Majority of people who win the lottery are back to where they started or worse within five years. This is true financially, but also emotionally. When you build your resources and assets to millionaire status, you learn how to manage the money. In addition to this, you learn how to deal with people who ask you for money or favors; you learn to decide which people and organizations you need to give to financially, which ones to build working relationships with, and which ones you should stay away from altogether. When you come into a large sum of money unexpectedly, there is no opportunity to learn these things. Oftentimes, people feel unworthy of the blessing or undervalue it. They don't think about investing. This is because it is easy to begin to spend it all superfluously. You don't know how to handle the stress from the calls from long lost friends and family members who are looking to you to solve all of their problems. As a result, the weight of the newfound responsibility can break a person.

Similarly, if God miraculously blessed you with a job as the CEO of a fortune five-hundred company, would you be able to manage it effectively in order for it to stay on top? Probably not, if you have only held lower or middle management positions and haven't spent time learning about the goals of the company. However, if He gave you a job right out of college at that same company, you would be able to develop the necessary skills that you would need in order to not only excel in that role, but advance in the company or potentially even start your own. What are you doing in your daily life that shows God that you can handle increase in your life? Are you falling apart any time something doesn't go your way? It is so important to study your craft, make your goals clear, and create clear steps to keep you going in the right direction. Be brutally honest with yourself about what you can do better. This is not to condemn yourself, but to hold yourself accountable. The situation may seem like it will never get better, and you may not see God working on your behalf. However, once you are in motion, you will be ready for the blessing that God gives.

Consider it this way, if God were to bless you with everything that you wanted or what you feel the "end game" is right now, would you feel like it is a curse? Now, of course the immediate reaction is "No, of course not!!" However, if you went from being single and working full time as an entry-level employee, to being a wife, a mother, and a power player in your career overnight, after one week, feelings of being overwhelmed and stressed would likely take over. You didn't have time to learn how to balance career responsibilities with family time, and date nights. We're not even going to mention alone time! In this situation, it would be easy to feel that the blessing was a burden. It'd feel like a burden because the focus would be on what used to be and how things were. The free time and the ability to be spontaneous would be missed. Yet, right now, it is easy to feel anxiety because the focus is on the future and what more could be done if everything worked perfectly the way we want it. This is why it is so important to focus on the present. Know your goals, but your focus should be on God and where He has placed you in this season.

What are all the things that bother you about where you are? What can be learned from these things to promote personal growth? How can you use what you have in abundance right now? Whether that is time, passion, health, etc., apply it to the desires that God has placed in your heart. It is going to require work. It demands intentionality. No amount of wishing will be enough. Passively waiting for the situation to be made perfect will have you waiting forever. More than likely, you won't finish. The tenacity that is gained through fighting for purpose is not something that can be achieved any other way. Seek God for guidance, then be confident in His plan. Remember, not everyone will understand your decision, but this is your life. You have a right to do what you are called to do. You also have a responsibility to do so. You'll never know the countless ways your gifts can help other people as long as you continue to put it off.

CHAPTER 13

Permission

"For they loved the praise of men more than the praise of God."

John 12:43 KJV

I just want to start this section off by giving a clear and simple public service announcement. To the person who is reading the book: I love you, and I want to remind you of the simple fact that if you are over the age of eighteen, you are an adult — even more so if you have left your parent's house. While giving respect to those in authority as well as others in general is important, it is necessary to remember that you absolutely do not have to ask for permission to do anything in your life. People like to try to thrust themselves as an authority figure in your life. It is your responsibility as a recovering good girl to politely show them to the theoretical door. No one on this earth knows your life and your business like you do, except for those select few people who you have shared those dreams. So anybody outside of that select few, cannot provide useful feedback for you in your situation. Because they don't understand the situation, they try to "protect" you by giving you misguided information and unsolicited advice. Others, especially people who are parental types, will feel the need to express their "disappointment" in you. Regardless, stand strong in the convictions that God has given you.

The purpose that you were called to fulfill won't make sense to a lot of people because they cannot understand the depth and scope of the calling. They cannot see the implications long term. Therefore, out of their personal fears and/or because of their overcautious natures, they attempt to pull you back to safety. You do not need the permission, validation, or affirmations of any other person in this world to confirm to you what you know God has said to you. You are free to have radical, unwavering, seemingly irrational faith in God. Choose to give it everything that you have. Once you do, you'll see that God will do incredible things with the sacrifice and the gift that you gave Him. At the point of success, the naysayers who were distracting you and trying to convince you to jump ship will be the same people asking you how in the world you succeeded. Do not require the praise and validation of people to the point that you are disconnected from your faith. Don't doubt the truth that the Lord has placed in your heart.

I stress this so much because most good girls constantly seek validation to ensure that they are doing the right thing at the right time. Unfortunately, the validation is usually sought from people who don't know any more about the issue than they do. In doing so, they are not actively pursuing the dreams that God has given them because they are waiting for someone to tell them that it's okay to do. Know that the validation that you seek may never come, and people may be uncomfortable with the risks that you are willing to take. However, by the time you convince them, you may have missed your moment. You have to be able to make a decision and own it whether or not you receive the affirmations that you desire. Better yet, it's probably better to stop asking every person in your life for their opinion, and just trust God's word.

Take for example the story of Mary and Martha when Jesus came to their home. Martha set out to do what was expected of her as a woman using society's standard of hospitality at that time. In other words, she was a good girl just following the rules. Mary, on the other hand, chose to sit at the feet of Jesus and listen to what He had to say. I'm sure everyone was surprised at that! Women didn't hang out with men socially, especially when there was housework to be done. I imagine that Martha was making a ton of noise in the kitchen, banging pots and pans, and being passive aggressive about her annoyance. In the moments of silence, she was probably straining to overhear what Jesus was saying. I'm sure she was more than a little jealous that Mary was bold enough abandon her chores to hang out with the guest in the living room, chatting about the true meaning of life. So since misery loves company, she tried to get Jesus to tell Mary to help her. I imagine her thinking, *if Jesus says it, then she's gotta do it.* What happened next probably shocked her. Jesus said no. He even called her *troubled,* then praised Mary for making the right choice. Jesus was pleased with the woman who put aside her earthly obligations in order to seek Him. (Luke 10:38–42)

If Mary would have waited for Martha to give her permission to make that bold decision, she would have died waiting. Martha did not have the foresight to really know who they were hosting in their home. She didn't value the opportunity that she had to sit at the feet of Jesus. Mary would have lived her entire life wondering what she could have learned had she just listened to Him the evening He decided to come. Instead, she seized her opportunity, and became a permanent example of God's expectation of us as well as an example of the pleasure He gets when we choose to abandon everything for Him.

Everyone who reads this story feels like they would be Mary. Of course, *we* would be the ones bold enough and carefree enough to break the mold and live in the moment. Nobody wants to be the uptight person who is stuck in ritual and custom and misses an opportunity of a lifetime. But, let's be real. Most of us are afraid of being different. We may experiment a little with fashion or our musical tastes, but when it comes to the core of who we are, most times we play it safe. We do what we are supposed to do, and we criticize the people who dare to behave unconventionally. The people who think, dress, and act outside of society's norm are the ones that receive the most disparagement. Sometimes this is because their choices make us uncomfortable. The fact that they are confident being different is a foreign concept to us, so we assume that something must be wrong with them. At other times, we are envious of their freedom. We wish that we were bold enough to live life without having anxiety about how others will feel about our decisions. However, since that doesn't seem like a possibility, we just hate on people who can.

Instead of having bitterness built deep inside of your heart, recognize that you can also be free of the expectations of others. It is as simple as making the decision to do so. It is the same as trying out a new hairstyle; if you wear it with confidence, most people won't have the audacity to say something directly to you about it. If they talk about you behind your back, maybe it's a good thing. You have finally given them something to talk about. I would also like to mention that, in reality, most of the expectations are in our heads. Your parents and close friends may have real expectations, and we will get to that in a moment, but for the most part, no one is really paying that much attention to you. They are busy having the same concerns as you are about themselves. Also, it's fine if people have opinions of you, right or wrong, because they are inconsequential. Who cares if they are mad, if you are living the life God designed? You don't need permission to follow the path that God laid out for you. Moreover, if you are worried about their opinions more than God's purpose for you, maybe you should check your priorities.

It is likely that your family and close friends do have expectations of you. While they love you and want what's best for you, they also love the role that you currently play in their lives. This is not a bad thing by any means. People get comfortable with the status quo so it is only natural that the things that you have continually done up to this point, they will want you to continue doing. In addition to this, because they love you, they don't want you to experience the hurt or rejection that may come from you stepping out on your own. They know that the standard route that everyone else follows is safe and requires no risk, and they think you will be content in this life. The thing is, it is your risk to take. You are the one who has to live with the regret of not living to your fullest potential. You are the one who will be wondering what could have been. Furthermore, even though your role in their lives may have to shift as you begin to work toward your goals, people will adjust. There may be growing pains, but if they love you, they will figure out how to make it work.

Throughout the book of Matthew, Jesus tells people to leave their family, sell their possessions, and abandon their careers in order to follow Him. If you go to church faithfully, but you are more concerned about what church people say than doing what He has commanded you specifically to do, are you really following Him? People will not always understand your mission. In fact, most people will not understand the full picture until they see the end result. But, they can't see it, because it's not for them to do. God has not revealed it to them the way He has with you. It is not your job to get them on board so that you can continue without opposition. It is your job to be bold enough to stand on God's promise and operate in faith until it comes to completion. They will get the revelation when it's time. But you are responsible for what you did with the information when you get it.

Really take this to heart. After reading this section, I hope you are convinced that you don't need approval from people. If you aren't, I hope that you spend some time thinking about why God's opinion doesn't have the final authority in your life and if you are willing to forgo your destiny for someone else.

Limitless

> *"But as it is written, Eye hath not seen, nor ear heard, neither have entered into the heart of man, the things which God hath prepared for them that love him."*
>
> 1 Corinthians 2:9, KJV

It's sad that the only thing that is natural for people to put limits on is themselves. We believe in society's ability to make positive social changes. We believe that technology will continue to advance and make our lives even simpler. It is easy for us to encourage others to go for their dreams. Yet, as soon as it comes to fulfilling our individual purpose, we have so many excuses as to why we can't succeed. Don't fall for the lie! When you are a child of God, there are literally no limits to what you can accomplish when you walk in purpose. Of course, that sounds good in theory, but some version of that phrase has been shared so much that they no longer carry the same weight in our spirit. However, it really is the truth.

If you don't believe that you are limitless, then you have accepted some limiting beliefs to be fact. You don't have enough money? You don't have the skills? You think that you will never be able to break the record? These false statements become real to you, when that is what you choose to believe. Really think about the internal dialogue when a challenge arises. What words are you using to describe the situation? Spoken words are powerful. When you hear yourself state things matter-of-factly, your mind believes it, and it becomes a law in your life. *"For as he thinketh in his heart, so is he..."* (Proverbs 23:7a, KJV)

So what would make us believe the reality of being limitless then? Change your thoughts. When you hear yourself say that you are unable to do something, correct yourself. Challenge the idea. In that moment, choose to think of the opportunity to do something that disproves the thought. Take the first step as an act of faith toward doing the impossible, or at least the highly improbable to start. Start speaking the dreams that have been deeply tucked away. If it is too soon to share with a close friend, then start by saying it aloud in the mirror. Dreams will always seem impossible if you are too afraid to even say what it is. Once you get comfortable saying it, your mind adjusts. It no longer seems unattainable. There is a shift, and you begin to think about what you can do in order to get closer to making the dream a reality.

Think about the last time that you accomplished a huge goal. Maybe it was graduating and earning the degree that you spent years working toward. Maybe it was getting an amazing and highly competitive internship or job. In the beginning, before you applied for it, you'd have to believe at least a little that you would get it. Then, the more you believed that you had a chance to succeed, the more effort that you would put into the work because you were excited to see the results. The best results come when you really believe that you can succeed — even in the beginning.

Boundaries

"No" is a complete sentence. So are "It's not happening," and "Stop asking." One of the most widespread misconceptions is that people deserve to know why. Most of us would like to know the answer, but you don't have to justify your reasoning to people who don't pay your bills. If answering their one question turns into twenty more, tell them to stop asking, or just walk away.

It can be extremely difficult to decide to create boundaries and even harder to enforce them. This is because many of us have been conditioned to think that it is rude to do so, especially if the person is well meaning. If they ask a question, we feel obligated to answer. Saying no seems rude and harsh to most people who are used to being overly accommodating, but you need boundaries in every area of your life. You should have a standard for the way that you expect to be treated.

Additionally, it is necessary that you qualify the advice that you are given. Just because she's a great hair dresser doesn't mean that she can tell you whether or not you should go forward you're your start-up ideas. When the person who is asking is an authority figure in your life, it doesn't always feel like you have the right to withhold information. However, it's not rude; it's wise. You are allowed to protect the ideas and plans that are still processing. Once the ideas have been developed and are ready to be shared, you'll gladly tell all who need and want to know. This isn't to distance you from them. It is to give you the ability to focus on what God has told you to do without any input that may stall your progress.

If you have never set boundaries before, people will more than likely keep pressing until they are heard. You have to hold your ground consistently over time. After a few times, people will realize that you have changed. They will either respect it, or slowly they'll drop out of your life. It sounds harsh and extreme that setting boundaries may cost you some relationships, but the people that leave never really respected you. They enjoyed what you did for them. Everyone who loves you will adapt. It is really that simple.

Not everyone can know your plans. Unfortunately, too many of us sit around answering back to back questions about our goals and dreams. By the end of the Q&A session, the other person has either completely discouraged us or deposited seeds of doubt that eventually stall your plans altogether. Most people won't understand your bold decisions. You have to remember that they don't really know you. They know the cookie cutout version of you that you showed them. So they aren't able to connect the dots between who they believe you are and who you really are, much less your vision for where you're going. In addition, the majority of people are unable to really look at situations from perspectives other than their own. They are looking through the lenses of who they are and why your decision would not work for them. So although they may mean well, the advice that they give is not applicable. Still, the doubt that they have lingers long past the conversation.

If you are doing something that is a completely new idea, it is even harder for people to understand. So don't answer their series of questions. Don't even give them enough information to ask the question. Safeguard your dreams. This is not being selfish; it is loving yourself enough to give your goal a real shot at coming to life. Remember at the end of your life, you are responsible for what you accomplished. All of the people that put doubt in your mind and encouraged you to have a "safe" life will be drowned out by the overwhelming disappointment that you didn't have the courage to do it anyway.

Keep in mind that boundaries are not only established to protect your ideas and goals, they also teach people how to treat you. Good girls are taught to be meek and humble, don't ask for much, and be happy with what you're given. Typically, after years or even decades of being a good girl, the people around you feel like they can say or do anything to you and you'll accept it. You are not a confrontational and refuse to correct their unacceptable behavior because it's not seen as ladylike, but God never intended for any of His children to be doormats. There is a way to be graceful yet firm.

Think of the last time you were asked out by a random guy on the street that you were not interested in dating. No matter how nicely he tried to ask for your number, as gently as you could, you rejected his offer. You were not rude; you were just being true to yourself. It was not because he was a bad guy, but because you know yourself and you know that he was not what you needed or wanted at that time. Whether the guy accepted your answer graciously, or he got upset and insulted you after he was rejected, you stuck with your original answer and continued with your day. However, when we deal with family and friends, many times, we burden ourselves with the anger and disappointment that they feel after we turn them down.

A huge misconception that good girls have is that if the person is nice, or they mean well, you have to accept what they have to offer. That just isn't true. If someone asks you to participate in a program that they are putting on, but it will take a substantial amount of time away from working on your projects that need to get done, you don't have to say yes. It is nice to help people when you can, and it's even nicer to go out of your way to help someone else. However, you also have to make time for your own needs. It doesn't make you a bad person to choose to be an active participant in your own life. You have to value yourself and your purpose before anyone else will.

Of course, it's not always that people are intentionally trying to disrespect you as a person. In fact, most times they are not. However, it may come in the form of someone who constantly wastes your time. They know that you will wait an hour after the designated time you were supposed to meet, so they are late every time. A friend who loves to complain will continue to rehash old problems over and over again even though you have already given them advice or encouragement on the issue several times. Sometimes you even have friends or relatives who continually ask for money for things they could have avoided, like parking tickets or bills when they've spent their money on extra clothes and eating out. You are more than a cash cow to bail them out of their recurring bad choices. Setting boundaries reminds people of your worth. The way that people adapt to your boundaries will show you whether or not they respect your feelings and decisions.

CHAPTER 14

Guilt

*"And another of his disciples said unto him, Lord, suffer
me first to go and bury my father. But Jesus said unto him,
Follow me; and let the dead bury their dead."*

Matthew 8:21–22, KJV

When people finally break out of their comfort zones and decide
to follow their dreams, they develop feelings of guilt. It tends to
come from family or friends who continue to mourn the loss of the
person you used to be by trying to insist that you go back. They are
uncomfortable and maybe even hurt by the change and want the
version of you that they knew and loved. Good girls don't intend to
hurt people, and it hurts them to know that they have caused pain.
In that transitional period, they often struggle with whether or not
they made the right decision. They consider appeasing their family
and friends by assisting them in some other way or compromising
their goals by settling between the life that you want and the life
that they loved. I consider this type of guilt a form of survivor's
remorse. Choosing to make a positive change for your future
should not make anyone feel bad, especially you. Sometimes there

have been real traumas in the past that create these feelings. If this is the case for you, absolutely talk to someone who can help you through it. However, some families and friends are upset simply because they miss you being in that specific role and want you to remain there only for their benefit with no consideration for what you need to do. Regardless, if God says it's time to move forward, you have to go. Everyone who loves you will adapt.

Keep pushing. Part of the reason that you feel this way about the situation is because they don't understand what you are doing. The other part likely stems from a little bit of doubt that is trying to get you to quit. Either way, continue to follow God's path. Don't allow yourself to focus on the past or people's current perception of you, because that is always relative. Just like it changed to make them feel this way, it can easily change again. Your life can't wait until they are ready. One man asked Jesus to be his disciple and follow after him, but he wanted to go home and bury his father first. Jesus made it clear, follow Him and let the dead bury their dead (Matthew 8:22, KJV). Their situation will work out even if you aren't there to fix it. God is omnipresent and omniscient. He can heal them and their situation and also guide you to yours. If it isn't what God is calling you to do right now, then it isn't your responsibility. Focus on what's ahead, and let God be God. What you are doing doesn't always make sense at the beginning, but the picture will be clear as day when you get there.

Forgiveness

"There is therefore now no condemnation to them which are in Christ Jesus, who walk not after the flesh, but after the Spirit."
Romans 8:1, KJV

Just like you can't limit or change yourself because of the way someone else views you, other people can't limit themselves to be only who you need or want them to be. It's okay. Forgive your family member or friend who can't see your goals, because it's a guarantee that not everyone will. In fact, most will not see the end results that you are working toward. Do not allow the shortsightedness of others to affect your end results. We've all heard some variation of this saying before — *Unforgiveness is like drinking poison and expecting the other person to die.* Whether the offense is a small social offense or a deep, traumatic and life changing event, forgiveness is one of the most amazing gifts that you can give yourself. Don't get me wrong, it is the legitimately one of the hardest things to do at times. The bigger the offense, the more you feel justified not forgiving. The people around you will validate your feelings and say that your resentment is understandable, but at the end of the day, it's still poisonous.

The anger, hurt, and frustration that you hold on to will continuously distract you from seeing where you are going because the only thing that you are focused on is the past. Sometimes, it is there for so long that it just becomes a part of who you are, and it becomes really difficult to get rid of on your own. Additionally, it hinders your ability to love completely or be vulnerable with new people. It stifles the ability to trust others. When you have lived an extended period of your life putting other people's needs before your own, it is easy to become bitter or resentful toward every new situation. The grudge becomes an excuse to doubt people's sincerity and opens the door to the fear of getting hurt. Inevitably, this causes people to be so closed off that they will not take a chance on anything significant. Bitterness will undoubtedly prevent you from reaching your full potential.

Your purpose is not to be average. You don't want to halfway fulfill your calling. Our God is incredible. If you are His child, made in His image, and He created you to fulfill His will, how can it be enough for you to be mediocre. It is so important that you let go of everything that keeps you mentally or emotionally bound. No individual thing you can accomplish will ever feel like a real achievement if you are still holding on to everything that has ever happened to you. You will never believe that your accomplishment is enough. The lingering feelings of inadequacy that cause you to second guess everything that you do are heavy burdens to drag with you through life. Holding onto the grievances that others have caused in your past experiences can evolve from general distrust to you entirely losing faith in God. You become unsettled, and you begin to fear situations where you are not in complete control. It's such an exhausting way to live. While the act of forgiving is not always the easiest thing to do, it is crucial to your future that you do it. In the long run, forgiving is a lot easier than carrying the weight of every person's transgressions with you for the rest of your life. Cut those weights, and give them to God so you can finish your race strong.

Growth is Expected

Moses led the children of Israel through numerous difficult situations from the time he returned to Egypt prepared to ask Pharaoh to allow them to leave captivity until his death. He saw God perform miracles regularly. At one point, the children of Israel were upset about not having water to drink while they were wandering through the desert (Exodus 17). So Moses prayed to God and asked for a solution because he feared the Israelites were ready to stone him out of their frustration. God gave him instructions to go to a specific rock and strike it. When he followed this instruction, God proved Himself again and provided water so that the needs of His people were met.

Years later, after Miriam had died, a similar situation arose. The people were thirsty and angry that they did not have access to water. Again, they complained and fought with Moses about it until he went to God again asking for a resolution. This time, God told him to speak to the rock in front of the crowd, and they will see the water come out at his command. When Moses got back to the children of Israel, he didn't speak to the rock as instructed. Instead, he struck it like he did the time before, probably mostly out of frustration. I can imagine that it also seemed crazy to him to speak to the rock in front of a crowd of angry Israelites. Even though striking a rock to get water doesn't make sense in the natural realm, he had done that before so it was a safe choice to do again. The water gushed out still, and there was enough for the people and their animals to drink. However, afterward, God told Moses that because he didn't trust Him to follow through with His commands, Moses would not be the one to bring the Israelites into the Promised Land. (Numbers 20:12)

Besides Joshua and Caleb, none of the Israelites, including Moses, made it to the Promised Land. God showed them miracles after miracles from their original exodus from Egypt to the daily manna for food. They had a cloud by day and a pillar of fire by night to guide them. Their clothes and shoes never wore out after decades of wandering through the hot desert. And they had fresh manna from heaven every morning. However, in spite of all of those things, they never really grew in their faith. They never let go of the fear of the unknown. They constantly wished to go back to their days of being slaves, because at least then they knew what to expect. That fear stunted their ability to grow in God. The miracles never empowered them to believe God for more. Because of it, they never saw the full promises of God. Since God cannot lie and had already promised that He would take the children of Israel into this land, He fulfilled his word by giving it to the next generation. God rescued them from slavery, but they still never got to experience the freedom that comes from believing in His promises.

When I was young, I heard these stories often in Sunday school and Bible Study classes. What I never understood was how they could see so many supernatural miracles and still worry about every little situation that came up. They didn't have to work for their food, and they definitely didn't have to worry about paying for rent and electricity. Literally, all they had to do was follow God's plan for the day. It seemed so easy. Then, I grew up. I faced various challenges and would start worrying about how I was going to make a deadline, pay a bill, and other transitional struggles that a lot of people go through. One day, while struggling to think of a solution, I had a revelation. I was reminded of all of the miracles that God provided me in my personal life, including several that literally saved my life. Then, I realized how easy it is to forget all of the blessings in your life when you are only focusing on the current problems. I was so convicted by it because it was easy to look at this example and judge them for not having faith in God after all He'd done for them. However, we rarely realize how similar we are to them in our behavior toward God. We have to make a conscious effort to remember the blessings of God, so when new issues arise, we have the faith to handle it.

The reason that God blesses us is because He genuinely loves and cares about us unconditionally. Yet, a side effect of experiencing those blessings is that we should be able to easily trust God with more. For most of us, it requires that we let go of situations that are out of our control, because we know that God is able to handle it. He has already proven Himself to be faithful by consistently providing blessings in our lives in so many different ways. We shouldn't be worried about the future. With every new obstacle that appears, remember that it is not a surprise to God. He is well aware of everything that is going to happen in your life, and He already has a plan to lead you through it. See the struggle as an opportunity for God to do something extraordinary. Challenge the fear by recalling the blessings of the past. God expects for us to be constantly growing in our relationship with Him. It is through our faith that He is able to provide miraculous solutions and opportunities in our lives.

CHAPTER 15

Faith

"A man's gift maketh room for him,
and bringeth him before great men."

Proverb 18:1, KJV

Now that we have talked about being authentic and intentional, we have to address whether or not we actually have faith. Faith is the ability to see and act on, ideas and beliefs that are not commonly understood, unseen, and seemingly illogical on the surface. Often times, faith feels like walking down a pitch black hallway, feeling the walls for guidance and hoping to reach the exit door where there's light on the other side. Even after your eyes start to adjust to the darkness, it can be hard to see the full picture. This is why it is so uncomfortable to operate in faith. We like tangible, physical proof. Believing in the unseen seems crazy. We all want a detailed, step by step, plan that has been notarized by God Himself. We want God to prove to us that it will work before we take any steps forward. Of course, would never say that, but most of the time our actions scream disbelief. Why else would we be waiting for the right time before we begin? What would you like to see to know that the right time has come?

As I mentioned in earlier sections, it will never seem perfect on paper; it requires faith. Always. The only things that don't require faith are the things that have already been done. Do you believe that you will become successful living in purpose? Can God really do anything? Of course we have faith in God's promises...right? Well, real faith is displayed through actions. We know that faith without works is dead, useless, and worthless. (James 2:26) So what are you doing consistently to show that you believe? If you knew without a shadow of a doubt that the next time your friend came over, they were bringing you a puppy that would be your new pet, there are certain things that you would do to prepare for it. You would invest in a food and water bowl, determine where it will sleep, and buy a doggie bed. It is just common sense. You'd take steps to get everything in order because you want to be prepared before the dog gets there.

Similarly, if we *know* that God is about to open doors for us and pour out blessings, we should be preparing for them. If you are an entrepreneur, do you believe that God will grow your customer base or that the next venture will be profitable? If you do, are you increasing your inventory so these people will have products to purchase? Have you trained your staff on how to operate in excellent customer service, so the new customers will share their positive experiences with their friends and families? You may need to hire an accountant who specializes in that level of revenue flows.

You should be actively learning and setting things in order in faith that blessings are on the way. Too often we err on the side of caution, which is really because we have doubts that we can excel. Society has given us this *hope for the best, plan for the worst* mentality. Out of fear you don't give it one hundred percent just in case it doesn't work out. Meanwhile, you are not realizing that it's not working out because you didn't give it all that you've got. So many people are halfway expecting their project to fail, and then get upset when it does. You have to run the race at full speed if you expect to have a shot at winning. If you are jogging because you don't think you can win, you guarantee that you won't win. When you are running your race at full speed, you can't think about anything other than making it to the finish line. You can't worry about how other people are running their race, and you definitely can't look around to see what else is happening in the stadium. All that matters is that you are running your race as best as you can.

> *"The blessing of the Lord, it maketh rich,*
> *and he addeth no sorrow with it."*
> Proverb 10:22, KJV

God doesn't give you more than you can handle. This is true for sorrow as well as success. Premature blessings can become burdens. Increases, especially in wealth, given to people who are not financially literate and disciplined, can cause those people to end up in even worse financial situations than they were in originally. Look at the lottery and game show winners. Many end up with the same amount of money or less than they had originally after only a few years. Hundreds of thousands, if not millions, of dollars are squandered because they were not prepared to invest the funds that they received. This is why many people do not get what they pray for right away. You have not prepared yourself to be able to handle it successfully. If we're being completely honest, are we even taking care of the blessings that we already received? Most of the things that we have right now are things that we used to pray for. Now that we have it, we take it for granted. We just want more. It is okay to want for more. God wants more for you. However, you have to prove that you are a good steward over what you have already, and then put the work into your faith in order to prepare for what's next. You have to evaluate yourself and see if God could really trust you to handle what you desire.

Another personal inventory check would be to see if you are just sabotaging yourself. If you are afraid of going to the next level, you may be holding on to negative behaviors, thought patterns or people that you should have gotten rid of long ago. It is common for people to self-sabotage as a self-defense mechanism. People that don't fully believe that they can be successful on a large platform or long term, sometimes will avoid failing by never really trying. They are afraid of the unknown. They would rather that the dream remains complacent than to have it fly high, and then worry about a potentially public crash and burn later. Even if they do believe in all of their heart that they will excel to a greater level of success, they don't know how they are going to handle it. They don't know what they will do once all of their current goals have been achieved.

Overall, they are simultaneously afraid of success and failure. It's insanity. If you did crash and burn, you would have that irreplaceable feeling of flying high for the rest of your life — even, if you only flew for just a few seconds. In addition, having to create more goals after accomplishing all of yours is literally the best problem that you could possibly have. Still, these are genuine concerns for a lot of people. Researching your goals and deciding to spend time preparing for your future will alleviate the majority of those concerns. Even if the fear persists, having faith means deciding to do it anyways. It comes down to a simple question. Will you operate in fear or in faith? Whichever one you choose to focus on will grow, but only one will leave you fulfilled at the end of your life.

Naysayers

There is an old proverb that says, "The person who says it cannot be done shouldn't interrupt the person doing it." Inevitably, when you start being intentional about making life changes, people will come out of the woodworks to tell you why what you're doing is not going to work. They will give you alternative or better plans, and encourage you to spend time creating a back-up plan. You have to determine which people around you can be trusted with your dreams. Sharing with the wrong people, or even sharing with the right people too soon, gives people the opportunity to plant seeds of doubt and potentially derail your plans before they even had a chance to succeed.

Caring for your dreams is like attempting to grow a plant successfully in a pot on the windowsill. There are good seeds in the soil, but you have to ensure that the soil remains properly watered. You have to make sure that there is enough sun and that soil itself has the nutrients that these seeds need to grow. If you forget to water it, the plant starts to droop. If this continues for too many days or it's taken out of the sun, it will start to wilt. However, if the plant is taken care of and is allowed to blossom, it will begin to outgrow the pot that it's in, and it will need a bigger pot. After a while, it will need to be planted in the yard so that it can continue to grow. The seed has that potential to be a huge fruit bearing plant whether or not it is ever planted. However, it is impossible to tell how fruitful the plant will grow just by looking at the seed. The work is required so that the plant is able to grow to its full potential.

Preparing for your dreams requires the same level of care. You have to do your research to learn everything that you need to know in order to get to the next level. You have to put in the work so that every day your dream is being nurtured. Foster an environment for growth. You have to protect the dream from people who may try to tear it down, and stay in the presence of people who wish to see you succeed. You may ask yourself why people would discourage you to follow your dreams? Isn't that the basis of America? Well, not many people are rude or hateful enough to tell you outright that you can't achieve your dreams. If asked directly, most people would say that they support you one hundred percent, and they want you to achieve everything that you are working toward. This is probably true for the most part. Though, people really are not that fond of change. When you begin to make major changes in your life, it challenges the people around you. They think, if you grew up together and have the same ideology why are you doing something different. They wonder if you think they need to change, too. Even though your growth has nothing to do with them, their insecurities begin to show through.

For example, if a person in South Texas decided that she wanted to become an ethical vegan. Let's say that she tells her friends and family who either try to discourage her or simply mock her choices. They perceive an element of rejection because this girl decided to eliminate the smoked barbeque that she was raised on from her diet completely. By extension, they may feel like she is rejecting her family and the culture itself. In addition to this, her friends and family fear that because of her decisions, she will one day expect them to also become vegan. They may have unwarranted concerns for her health, or they may simply not know how to cater to her dietary needs anymore and feel uncomfortable at meals with her. Those are very real concerns. However, it is not the responsibility of the person who is making the change to make sure that everyone is comfortable before she begins her journey of what is right for her. She'd probably never start if that were the case. Her family would just assume it was a fad and disregard it altogether. By continuing, in spite of the baggage of those around her, she is able to lead by example, and she has the opportunity to show them another way of life.

The first thing that I ever wanted to be was an author. I have loved reading since I learned as a little kid. Before I was taught to read, I would pretend like I could read and guess what the words said by the picture on every TV commercial and billboard that I saw. Once I got into school, everyone realized how good I was at math and the sciences. All through school and college, I was encouraged to concentrate my focus in STEM classes. Yet, even though I was really good at it and I understood the concepts, it was not something I really enjoyed. It bored me. I wanted to be an entrepreneur and an author, but I was constantly encouraged to continue in mathematics because of the endless opportunities for a woman in STEM. However, after I graduated Summa Cum Laude, distinction in the field with my mathematics degree, I didn't even want to consider further schooling in the field. I realized that I now I had a degree to do something that I never wanted to use in a career. I had allowed all of these well-meaning, good-hearted people tell me what they thought was best for my future because I respected them. I didn't trust my own convictions, and I didn't realize that it bothered me so much because my spirit disagreed with me preparing for a future that God did not prepare for me.

Unfortunately, this is not all that uncommon. It is natural for us to seek the validation of our parents and teachers. What's unnatural is walking in faith. There are so many times when the road to purpose does not seem like the road to success. There are lots of surprises, twists, and turns, and it involves a lot of hard work. However, the path and the destination are both extremely rewarding. Meanwhile, there are other paths that appear to be so much more fun on the surface. It seems easier to attain success, and it includes the validations of family and friends. While these paths may look great on paper, they do not provide any meaningful level of satisfaction. They don't even lead to the ultimate dream, so there will always be something missing. Taking this path is choosing to live your own Plan B life instead of trusting God for His best that

He planned for you. Only you know the desires that God placed deep inside of you. Other people can only offer advice based on what they have seen. You have to seek God and trust in His word for yourself. It is the only way for you to be victorious in life.

CHAPTER 16

Fly

In the New Testament, Holy Spirit is compared to a dove. He is often characterized by the wind. These representations are symbolic of how free and limitless He is. "Where the Spirit of the Lord is, there is liberty." (2 Corinthians 3:17b, KJV) We have access to that free nature when He abides in us. So fly as high as you can. Leave the doubts, fears, and anxieties to fall to the ground as you take flight. The only thing stopping you is yourself. Release yourself from the expectations of others, and allow yourself to believe that you can do incredible things. View life from a new vantage point. There is literally no obstacle that is too big. The wind can go anywhere. You can be exceptional. Don't settle for just being good, girl.

You Have Everything to Lose

When looking at a new product at the store, it is common to hear marketers encourage people to try it because, *you have nothing to lose*. That might be true for trying a new skin care line, but when it comes to your destiny, I believe that you have everything to lose. Product marketers are focusing on comparing your future potential pleasure to your past dissatisfaction. Your tomorrow might be better than today. However, complacency may cause you to believe that the level of satisfaction in your present life is good enough. So I compare the future that you are projected to have by continuing a life of passivity to the future that you would have by living a life of faith. The two are worlds apart. The decision to delay or dismiss working toward destiny can have devastating effects on the future that God desires you to have. On top of that, His destiny is always much bigger and more satisfying than anything that we could ever imagine. You have everything to lose.

In Matthew 25, Jesus shares a parable of the talents. A man was going away on a trip and expected his servants to take care of his property and possessions. Before leaving, he gave each of three servants talents, units of currency, according to what they were capable of handling: one five, one two, and the last received one. The first two servants doubled the owner's investment and when the owner returned they were able to present him with it. When they did, the master celebrated them, invited them to his feast, and gave them greater responsibilities. They had shown him that they could be trusted with more. Then, the final servant came forward. He told the master that he didn't want to take the risk of losing the money. He basically said the master was so good at being successful, even when everyone else failed, he didn't want to get in the way of his success. Instead, he just buried the talent while the master was away. This way there was absolutely no risk, and he could return it upon the master's arrival. The master was furious. If the servant knew that he always turned a profit, why wouldn't he go forward with the investment? The servant wasted the investment that he'd made. The master took the one talent that he had back, and gave it to the servant that doubled his talents to ten. Then, the servant was thrown into the abyss. (Matthew 25:14–30)

I can imagine the mindsets of each of the servants while the master was away. The one with five was probably excited that he was trusted with so much and immediately began thinking of ways to turn a profit. The servant with two talents probably was a little insecure because he wasn't given five. He didn't have as much to work with and had little room for error. However, he saw the excitement of the guy with five and decided that he was going to go for it. This was his opportunity to show the master that he, too, could be trusted with five talents next time he was away, and he wasn't going to miss it. I imagine the last servant looking at the other two as if they'd lost their minds. This man that we work for is hard and strict, and if you lose even a dime of that talent, he will punish you severely. They may be crazy enough to play with his money, but I only have one. There's no way in the world I'm risking losing the only talent that I was given. Let me hide it so no one can even steal it from me.

This reminds me of so many conversations that I have overheard or even been a part of in my lifetime. *Of course this person was successful because they're literally good at everything.* Or *I don't have the money that they have so I don't want to waste it in case it doesn't turn out the way that I hoped it would.* However, even if you feel like you were not given a lot of opportunities, gifts, or talents, you are still responsible for returning a profit from the things that you do have. What many people call erring on the side of caution is really just squandering God's investments. Faith pleases God, not caution. The last servant didn't realize that because the master always turned a profit, it bettered his odds. He didn't have the same limitations as ordinary people. This talent was blessed. Unfortunately, because he failed to realize this and take advantage of this opportunity, it costed him not just his talent, but also his job and likely his life as well.

Hindsight has perfect vision. The regret of knowing that you missed your opportunity to drastically change your life is a huge weight to bear. Wondering what could have been is not worth the temporary satisfaction of feeling safe. Think of all things that you would go back in time to change if you could already. Those things probably are just embarrassing or stupid things that you did as a teenager. How much more will you regret not taking this time to fulfill your calling? You don't want to add to that number by continuing this pattern of passivity in your life. Now is the perfect time to act in order to prevent future regrets. It is the only time to act. We don't know what the future holds, so this is the moment to choose to be great. Greatness does not guarantee that you will be a billionaire, but it does mean that your life will be fulfilled and full of purpose. Experiencing greatness is literally experiencing God's favor on your life. It is an insatiable feeling because you know that God always has more for you even after every milestone has been accomplished.

At the end of the day, it does come down to choice. In the moment of the decision, will you choose to put in the effort that is required, or will you watch a few hours of TV instead? If, out of habit you realize that you have watched movies for a few hours after getting home from work, will you decide to turn the TV off and make the most of the time that you have left that evening? Or, will you just continue to put it off until tomorrow? The now can seem terrifying. In it, you are immediately confronted by the grandness of the dream itself. Sometimes you are even overwhelmed. You have to stand up to the fear and other obstacles that have been overtaking your life for years, but it can be so exhilarating as well! Each accomplishment comes with this proud mama moment because you made progress on something that you have always wanted to do. You've finally crossed something off the Life List, and you learn how strong and resilient you can be. Push past the anxiety and inch your way toward success until you can crawl. Take those few wobbly first steps. Before you know it, you'll be sprinting so fast that it feels like the dream itself is running toward you! It all starts with the choice in the moment.

In all honesty, when you think about it, it isn't even that much of a risk. It is common for people to experience hard times in their everyday lives anyways. That is not exclusive to people living a life of faith. It's quite possible that you feel misunderstood, underappreciated, or alone already. So basically, you are experiencing the same negative side effects that you fear are included in living a life of faith and are trying to avoid. Just think about that for a moment. In theory, if it was true that you were going to feel those things regardless, you may as well be living a life of purpose, because right now you are just missing out on all of the perks! The reality is that many of those negative emotions will change.

In the process of actively working toward your goals, you lose the fear, the anxiety, and the doubt. Everything that was weighing you down before is lost once you choose faith. Living a life of faith frees the mind and the spirit. Worry does not exist in faith. Faith is able to accept more opportunities because they aren't immediately discounted due to fear of the unknown or the fear of failure. Again, you have everything to lose! I have quoted this before but it is worth reiterating, *"The blessing of the Lord, it maketh rich, and he addeth no sorrow with it."* (Proverb 10:22, KJV) *No sorrow!* Once you start walking in faith, things will align according to His purpose for you. You will have everything that you need. Just start. Try *something.* Keep going on faith until you start to see results. The situations that you experience will not always look perfect, but if you commit to living a life of faith and seek God every step of the way, it is impossible to fail.

Staying the same is easy. It requires no effort. You don't have to make any changes to your mindset or your lifestyles. You can choose to believe that life just happens to you and that you have no control over it. Because we were all given free will, you are able to live that life if you choose. You can continue to believe that you aren't worth the sacrifice or that you were destined to live a mediocre life, bound by the demands of everyone else. Or, you can decide to trust God's promise of "exceeding, abundantly" above all that you can even ask or think. (Ephesians 3:20, KJV) You have to decide if you want a life that is easy or one that is worth the effort. Again, effort doesn't mean that it has to be difficult and frustrating. It means that you have to choose to make advances in that area of your life. It indicates the intentionality in your life because every day you will make the decision to do be an active participant in life, instead of just a bystander in it. Choosing not to take any risks so that you won't make any mistakes is cowardly. Instead, choose faith. This is your opportunity to be free. This is the sign that you have been waiting for. You are one decision away from radically changing the course of your life. Unapologetically decide to be the person who God called you to be.

CHAPTER 17

Final Thoughts

"His lord said unto him, Well done, good and faithful servant; thou hast been faithful over a few things, I will make thee ruler over many things: enter thou into the joy of thy lord."
Matthew 25:23, KJV

We aren't guaranteed a specific amount of time on this earth. We have no idea when we will run out. Think of how many people in the history of the world have died before being able to fulfill their purpose. All of the potential advances in society legally, politically, technologically, as well as socially that we have missed out because people have passed away before they were able to fulfill their purpose. Think of the millions of ideas and plans, maybe even cures for diseases that left with those people. It is unfortunate for the whole world that the wealthiest place on the planet has become the graves. The only way to change this narrative is for the people who are still alive and full of potential to live their life being authentic, intentional, and unapologetic about working within their purpose.

It's not too late. Your current stage in life doesn't matter. You are still alive and breathing. You still have the opportunity to be more than *just* okay. You can be more than just average and just like everyone else. God given talent lives in you, and it won't stop nagging you until you step out on faith and take the risk. If God wanted you to be just like everyone else, He would have made you that way. Don't let your spirit die. Fight for your life. Stop sitting passively through life, waiting for it to be your turn to really live. It is your time right now, and you won't get a second chance to live this moment. Your life is valuable. Nothing is more precious than your time because you can never get it back. Therefore, you must use it wisely.

God created each of us with a purpose, so there is something deep inside of you that you desire to do. That longing will never go away. The longer that you wait, the deeper the regret that you will have that you haven't already done it. Not only that, too often the fear grows exponentially with each passing year. Unfortunately, most people become more conservative as they age, and putting it off will not make it any easier. Plus, now it seems like it's too late or you don't have the time, etc. The only way to avoid this is to be bold enough to take the leap of faith. It is called a leap for a reason. If you knew everything that was going to happen next, you would have done it already. If you are waiting for all of the pieces of the puzzle align perfectly, you will never do it. You have to jump. Be as prepared as you can be, and research your craft. But, at some point you have to jump. You will feel like you're flying for a while, and your stomach may drop from the fall. However, at the end of the day, you will fly because your gifts will make room for you. That is a guaranteed promise from God, so you really have nothing to lose. Choose an abundant, unimaginably fulfilling, purposeful, and vibrant God-filled life. That's what's on the other side of your hesitation. You don't have to just watch other people succeed while you wait for your turn. Set aside all of the excuses and choose to live for God. All it takes is a little faith and a bold decision. The situation may not change until you make the call.

I heard an interesting comparison that is great to remember when you start to feel bad about standing up for yourself and deciding to take care of your needs. On an airplane, the flight attendants tell the passengers that in the event that the air pressure changes in the cabin and the ventilating masks drop from overhead, put your mask on securely before you help others. If you go around the airplane putting on everyone's mask for them, you will likely faint or even die. You will not have enough air to sufficiently and properly secure the people around you. However, if you place your mask on first, you can help everyone within your reach. Just the same, it will literally kill your hopes and dreams if you spend your whole life doing things for other people at your own expense. It's great to help your family, and it's great to want to do right by your friends and your community. Still, don't forget the person that will be there your entire life. Love yourself, authentically. Take care of yourself, intentionally. Be strong enough, bold enough, and free enough to live life unapologetically. Live with the confidence of knowing who God created you to be, and walk your God-given authority. Good girls will never finish the race with all of the weights of other people's problems and expectations on their shoulders. Shake them off, and run your race. There's no more time to just be good, girl. Be great. Live your life full of faith. Decide to change your life, girl! For good.

God's Promise to You

You've just finished this book and hopefully you are inspired to live life differently. Don't let your mind give you anxiety or fear about your leap of faith. This is just a little reminder of the promise that God has given you. Take it personally!

Matthew 6:25 – 34, The VOICE

[25] *Here is the bottom line: do not worry about your life. Don't worry about what you will eat or what you will drink. Don't worry about how you clothe your body. Living is about more than merely eating, and the body is about more than dressing up.* [26] *Look at the birds in the sky. They do not store food for winter. They don't plant gardens. They do not sow or reap — and yet, they are always fed because your heavenly Father feeds them. And you are even more precious to Him than a beautiful bird. If He looks after them, of course He will look after you.* [27] *Worrying does not do any good; who here can claim to add even an hour to his life by worrying?*

[28] *Nor should you worry about clothes. Consider the lilies of the field and how they grow. They do not work or weave or sew, and yet their garments are stunning.* [29] *Even King Solomon, dressed in his most regal garb, was not as lovely as these lilies.* [30] *And think about grassy fields — the grasses are here now, but they will be dead by winter. And yet God adorns them so radiantly. How much more will He clothe you, you of little faith, you who have no trust?*

[31] *So do not consume yourselves with questions: What will we eat? What will we drink? What will we wear?* [32] *Outsiders make themselves frantic over such questions; they don't realize that your heavenly Father knows exactly what you need.* [33] *Seek first the kingdom of God and His righteousness, and then all these things will be given to you too.* [34] *So do not worry about tomorrow. Let tomorrow worry about itself. Living faithfully is a large enough task for today.*

Declarations

- ❤ I have everything that I need.
- ❤ I am a daughter of the Most High God.
- ❤ I have dominion over my situation.
- ❤ God's promises are true and they apply to my present life.
- ❤ I walk with confidence because God is with me.
- ❤ Let Your perfect will manifest in my life.
- ❤ And my best is yet to come!

Philippians 4:19, NIV

And my God will meet all your needs according to the riches of his glory in Christ Jesus.

Romans 8:16, NIV

The Spirit himself testifies with our spirit that we are God's children.

Psalm 8:6, NIV

You made them rulers over the works of your hands; you put everything under their feet:

Deuteronomy 7:9, NIV

Know therefore that the Lord your God is God; he is the faithful God, keeping his covenant of love to a thousand generations of those who love him and keep his commandments.

Deuteronomy 31:6, NIV

Be strong and courageous. Do not be afraid or terrified because of them, for the Lord your God goes with you; he will never leave you nor forsake you.

Mathew 6:10, KJV
Thy kingdom come, Thy will be done in earth, as it is in heaven.

1 Corinthians 2:9, KJV
But as it is written, Eye hath not seen, nor ear heard, neither have entered into the heart of man, the things which God hath prepared for them that love him.

Author's Note:

Hey girl! Thank you for reading this book. I hope you are encouraged in your journey to fulfilling your purpose here on earth. Sometimes we need someone to shake us so we realize the gravity of the situation at hand. We need people to challenge our limiting beliefs as well as the lies that we tell ourselves in order to remove ourselves from the responsibility of the assignment. This is for the good girl who, like me, dreamed of having more but was terrified to go after it. This is your time to do what you were created to do! Be Bold! Trust in God! And, know that you walking in faith pleases Him. Give God your best, and watch the miraculous ways that your life transforms.

With Love,

Felicia White

www.ingramcontent.com/pod-product-compliance
Lightning Source LLC
Chambersburg PA
CBHW072009090426
42740CB00011B/2147